# A Passion for the Past

## Historic Collections of Antiquities
from Egypt and the Levant

USHABTI FIGURE.

# A Passion for the Past

## Historic Collections of Antiquities
## from Egypt and the Levant

Norman Hurst

Hurst Gallery
Cambridge, Massachusetts

Text: Norman Hurst
Photography: Vernon Doucette
Design and layout: Jesse Taggert
Editing: Lara Greenwood and Nicole Hawkes
Project coordination: Lara Greenwood
Project assistance: Nicole Hawkes


Publisher:
Hurst Gallery
53 Mount Auburn Street
Cambridge, Massachusetts 02138

**FRONT COVER:** Isis holding Horus (cat. 53)

**BACK COVER:** Ptahtek amulet (cat. 52)

**FRONTISPIECE:** Shabty (cat. 25)

**INSIDE FRONT COVER:**
Three potsherds, Smith collection, labeled: *Samaria, 500;*
    *Jericho, 500; Aleppo, 47*
Limestone fragment with tag, Smith collection
26 Egyptian beads of various materials, Smith collection:
    *Bot of Dr. Banks, Mar 22, 1940 ($20)*
Tag from a shabty, Smith collection
Photograph from Endowment for Biblical Research
    archives: back row, from left to right: Esther S. Smith,
    Alma Lutz, Margaret Lutz Fogg, A. Marguerite
    Smith; front row: five dragomen [translators and guides]
    (Egypt, 1938)

**INSIDE BACK COVER:**
Shabty with tag and label (cat. 29)
Two clay cones from a group of seven (cats. 79–85)
Tag from a wooden servant figure (cat. 23)
Fragmentary spear point with label (cat. 1)
Egyptian necklace, ancient faience beads with modern
    stranding and clasp, Smith collection: *Sohag, 1908.*

# Hurst Gallery
53 Mount Auburn Street   Cambridge, Massachusetts 02138
TEL (617) 491-6888  FAX (617) 661-0439  E-MAIL hurst@world.std.com

# CONTENTS

## ACKNOWLEDGEMENTS

The author wishes to acknowledge the invaluable assistance of Mr. John A. Larson, Museum Archivist at the Oriental Institute of the University of Chicago, whose extraordinary knowledge and diligence have enabled reuniting biographical and other previously lost details with the collection histories of many of these objects. Ms. Ulla Kasten, Museum Editor of the Babylonian Collection, Yale University, has been very generous with her time in helping with translations and attributions of the Mesopotamian materials. I should also like to acknowledge the assistance of several Egyptian and Levantine scholars who wish to remain anonymous. Finally, the cheerful attention to preservation and transmission of the minutiae of data associated with the Smith collection, and the thoroughgoing appreciation of its significance evidenced by Mr. Stephen Howard, Administrative Executive of the Endowment for Biblical Research, Boston, have made work on this project a special pleasure.

The author sincerely thanks Ms. Lara Greenwood for her customary inspired editing and attention to detail; Ms. Nicole Hawkes for her diplomacy, level-headed management, and repeated ordering of chaos; Mr. Vernon Doucette for his sensitive photography; and Ms. Jesse Taggert for having the courage to undertake the design and production of another Hurst Gallery catalogue.

*Watercolor by Daphne Banks (daughter of Dr. Edgar James Banks)*

The objects presented here were collected between the 1860s and the early 1950s, a period marked by a florescence of American and European interest in Egypt and the Levant. Most come from important historic collections; some were excavated by well known archaeologists and others were collected *in situ* by 19th and early 20th century travelers.

The development of steamship and rail transportation and the completion of the Suez Canal in 1869 were factors which helped tens of thousands visit sites in Egypt, Mesopotamia, and the land of ancient Israel. In addition, the well-publicized work of archaeologists such as Gaston Maspero, W. M. Flinders Petrie, and Howard Carter stimulated interest among the diverse group of scholars, journalists, archaeologists, and tourists, whose collections are represented here. Two of the objects were actually excavated by Petrie in the late 19th century, another was acquired from the Cairo Museum in 1906, and yet another comes from the collection of William Tilden Blodgett, one of the founders of the Metropolitan Museum of Art.

The largest portion of these antiquities are from the collection of A. Marguerite Smith (1889–1959), who had more than a passing tourist's interest in Egypt and the Levant. As the librarian and a trustee of the Zion Research Foundation (later renamed the Endowment for Biblical Research, Boston) of Brookline, Massachusetts, Smith was committed to the study of biblical history. Her position brought her into close contact with many archaeologists and biblical scholars of her day. She acquired some of her objects at the time of her visit to the region in 1937–8, and until 1951 she continued to collect from European and American dealers, archaeologists, and other sources.

Smith's primary source was Dr. Edgar James Banks (1866–1945), a Mesopotamian archaeologist and the author of *The Bible and the Spade* and *Bismya, or the Lost City of Adab*. Although his specialty was not Egypt, Banks purchased a large collection of Egyptian objects from the British historian, Henry Buckle (1821–1862). In Egypt, shortly before his death, Buckle assembled a collection of over 600 ancient objects; the collection changed hands twice before Banks acquired it from an American owner in 1933. All of the Egyptian objects which Smith acquired from Banks probably came from this collection.

Smith also purchased many pieces from the Bodley Bookshop in New York. These objects came from various sources, some from celebrated collections, including that of F. G. Hilton Price, and some from famous people such as Consuelo Vanderbilt, Duchess of Marlborough; and Count Alexandre Florian Joseph Colonna Walewski, the son of Napoleon Bonaparte. Information about these collectors is included with the objects.

The author has tried to provide the complete collection history for every object presented here. Smith's meticulous, though sometimes cryptic, records, include the person from whom she purchased the object, the previous owners, and often the date of purchase and price paid; the text of her notes is reproduced with each item.

Hurst Gallery has always made a practice of thoroughly researching the provenance of each object and of dealing only with objects which, according to the best information available, have been transported in conformance with international regulations. It is a special satisfaction, therefore, to be able to offer these objects, which not only have their own intrinsic value, but also retain such well documented and, in some cases, historically significant, provenances. A portion of the proceeds from the sale of all of the objects from the Smith collection will benefit the Endowment for Biblical Research, a non-denominational charitable foundation.

–Norman Hurst

# Egyptian Art and Artifacts

Long before the beginning of the ancient civilizations from which the objects in this exhibition and catalogue derive, Egypt was home to Paleolithic peoples whose material culture remains are limited to stone tools. The Acheulian hand axe (cat. 2) is an example of one such implement, which has survived at least 250,000 years. The finished form was produced from a core stone by percussion flaking. For similar examples, cf. Scott (1986:23, cat.1b) and Spencer (1993:17, 18, pl.5).

During the Pre-Dynastic period (5500–3000 BC), Neolithic peoples dominated this region. Finely worked flint tools and weapons such as the concave-base arrowheads (cats. 3, 4) and the fragmentary knife blade (cat. 1) demonstrate the advancement of Neolithic technology. The blades were finished using a pressure flaking technique which allowed the craftsman to carefully control both the outline and bevel of the edge. The use of flint blades, especially in agriculture, coexisted with copper technology at least until the beginning of the New Kingdom, circa 1558 BC. For examples of concave-base arrowheads see Scott (1986:24, cat.2a, 2c) and Shick (in Celenko 1996:21–2, ill.5).

The flint blade (cat.1) was collected by W. M. Flinders Petrie during his work at Negadeh in 1894–5 and is of the type called a "fish-tail" knife; complete blades of this type exhibited a forked tang, which is missing here (for examples see Petrie 1896:fig.2:7, pl. LXXIII). These knives are thought to have had only ceremonial use; they were often ritually broken or "killed" and placed with the deceased (Harvey in D'Auria 1988:73). Although the precise funereal significance of these blades in the Pre-Dynastic period is uncertain, during the Old Kingdom, the form probably evolved into the *pesesh-kef* wand, which was used in the opening of the mouth ritual, "which awakened the deceased's facility of speech" (Ibid.:73). For examples and descriptions of *pesesh-kef* wands, see Roth (in D'Auria 1988:81,pl.11;224,pl.177b).

**1**
**Fragmentary spear point**
Probably early Gerzean (circa 3500 BC)
Chert
L: 4.5 in. (11.4 cm), W: 1.5 in. (3.8 cm)
Excavated by W.M.F. Petrie at Negadeh, 1894–5; Ex collection
Professor Paul Arthur, Archaeologist, University of Lecce, Italy
Ink notation: *A.*; paper label: [Illegible word] *1896, Negadeh,
W.M.F. Petrie, 1894–5*

**2**
**Hand axe**
Upper Acheulian (600,000–250,000 BC)
Chert
L: 5 in. (12.7 cm), W: 3.75 in. (9.5 cm)
Ex collection Sterling Callisen (1899–1988); Callisen traveled
extensively throughout his life as a museum administrator,
educator, and collector. Several objects from his collection
of Egyptian art are in the Metropolitan Museum of Art.

**3**
**Concave-base arrowhead**
Neolithic (5500–4300 BC)
Chert
L: 2 in. (5.1 cm), W: 1 in. (2.5 cm)
Ex collection Edward Budde, New York; Budde assembled an
impressive collection of arms and antiquites from Egypt and the
Levant in the 1940s and 50s.

**4**
**Concave-base arrowhead**
Neolithic (5500–4300 BC)
Chert
L: 2 in. (5.1 cm), W: 1.5 in. (3.8 cm)
Ex collection Edward Budde, New York

# STONE VESSELS

The Egyptian craft of stone cutting and carving is an ancient one; carved stone vessels show evidence of great expertise and skill from their first appearance in the earliest dynasties. This laborious process was initiated by roughly shaping quarried blocks of stone with chisels, then smoothing them with a sanding stone. Surviving unfinished vessels reveal that the exterior shape was first completed, then the vessel cavity was excavated using bits of varying sizes. A small stone-tipped bit was first used, then copper tubes were employed to extract cylindrical sections. Finally, round bits were used to complete the finished interior which, in the finest vessels, might be fully carved to conform to the shape of the exterior wall, producing an object of great delicacy.

Every available stone was used for containers of varied types; the favored stones were alabaster, serpentine, limestone, basalt, and breccia, all of which were naturally occurring in Egypt. In the early Dynastic Period, a large number of vessel types were made from a variety of materials, but by the end of the Old Kingdom, alabaster had replaced hard stone as the material of choice (Hayes 1978: 22, 23). Alabaster (*Crystalline calcium carbonate*) is a soft stone, ranging in color from white to creamy yellow. It is relatively easy to carve and polish; skilled stone cutters utilized the curves of its veining and the stone's translucence to create the finest of vessels. In addition to the alabaster vessels here, see the alabaster shabty (cat. 25).

Stone vessels were made in a wide variety of shapes and sizes, ranging from large canopic jars (containers for mummified organs) over a foot high, to miniature containers (cat. 13) a fraction of an inch tall, that would have held precious ointments or eye makeup.

Cats. 8, 10, 12, and 14 are examples of kohl pots from the New Kingdom. The ancient Egyptians used green, and most commonly black, kohl as cosmetic eyeliner. The use of beautifully grained or patterned stone for kohl pots is characteristic of the lavish taste of this period. According to Brovarski (in Brovarski 1982: 216–7), kohl pots of stone were made throughout the Middle Kingdom and in the New Kingdom through the reign of Thutmose III. Kohl pots raised on legs (cat. 10) were in vogue in the Middle Kingdom and those with a wide flat rim and carefully fitted lid such as cats. 8 and 14 typify those of Dynasty 18.

Judging from tomb paintings of banquets, the upper classes used stone containers for food, drink, and as serving dishes. The stone vessels were also used in temple rituals and funerary practices. Often, miniatures or models of regular sized vessels were placed in tombs for the use of the deceased in the next world (Hayes 1978: 118–20).

**5**
**Bowl**
Dynasty 3 (2686–2613 BC)
Steatite
H: 2.4 in. (6.1 cm), D: 7.4 in. (18.8 cm)
Ex collection Allen L. Owens, Connecticut; auctioned at Parke-Bernet Galleries, December 4, 1969, sale no. 2946, lot no. 49
Paper labels: *PB 49* and *V915*

**6**
**Cup with flared sides**
Dynasty 3 (2686–2613 BC)
Limestone
H: 3.25 in. (8.3 cm), D: 4.25 in. (10.8 cm)
Smith collection

**7**
**Alabastron**
Late Period (760–330 BC)
Alabaster
H: 8.75 in. (22.2 cm), D: 1.875 in. (4.8 cm)
Smith collection: *Bodley Dec. 26 '40, from Vose collection.*
No information has been discovered about the Vose collection.

**8**
**Kohl pot**
Dynasty 18 (1558–1303 BC)
Diorite
H: 2.3125 in. (5.9 cm), D: 2 in. (5.1 cm)
Smith collection: *From the Buckle collection, found near Memphis in 1862. Used in temples about the time of Moses. Bot of Dr. Banks, no. 105, Jan. 29, 1940 (50.–) Collection of 14 175.–*

### 9
**Small cosmetic bowl**
Middle Kingdom (2040–1633 BC)
Alabaster
H: 2.25 in. (5.7 cm), D: 1.625 in. (4.1 cm)
Smith collection: *From the Buckle collection, found in Memphis in 1862. Used in temples about the time of Moses. Bot of Dr. Banks, no. 107, Jan. 29, 1940 (15.–) Collection of 14 175.–*

### 10
**Footed kohl jar**
Second Intermediate Period (1786–1558 BC)
Alabaster
H: 1.375 in. (3.5 cm), D: 1.375 in. (3.5 cm)
Smith collection: *Buckle collection, found near Memphis in 1862. Used in temples about the time of Moses. Bot of Dr. Banks, no. 110, Jan. 29, 1940 (12–) Collection of 14 175.–*

### 11
**Shallow carinated bowl**
Early Dynastic to Old Kingdom (3100–2160 BC)
Alabaster
H: 1.625 in. (4.1 cm), W: 3.75 in. (9.5 cm)
Smith collection: *From Buckle collection, Bot of Dr. Banks, no. 100, Sept. 13, 1937 10.–*

### 12
**Kohl pot**
New Kingdom (1558–1085 BC)
Hematite
H: 1.375 in. (3.5 cm), D: 2 in. (5.1 cm)
Smith collection: *From the Buckle collection, found near Memphis in 1862. Used in temples about the time of Moses. Bot of Dr. Banks, no. 106, Jan. 29, 1940 (15.–) Collection of 14 175.–*

### 13
**Miniature vessel**
Late Period (760–330 BC)
Alabaster
H: 1.25 in. (3.2 cm)
Smith collection: *From Buckle collection, found near Memphis in 1862. Used in temples about the time of Moses. Bot of Dr. Banks, no. 111, Jan. 29, 1940 (10–) Collection of 14 175.–*

### 14
**Kohl pot**
Dynasty 18 (1558–1303 BC)
Steatite
H: 2.5 in. (6.4 cm), D: 2.5 in. (6.4 cm)
Condition: rim repaired
Smith collection: *Buckle Collection, found near Memphis in 1862. Used in temples about the time of Moses. Bot of Dr. Banks, no. 75, Jan. 29, 1940 15.–*

**15**
**Cylindrical beaker**
Dynasty 1 (3100–2890 BC)
Alabaster
H: 6.25 in. (15.9 cm), D: 4.25 in. (10.8 cm)
Condition: rejoined
Smith collection: *Bot of Dr. Banks Oct. 12, 1937 15.–*

This beaker is made of a fine grained gray alabaster; the shape was
common in royal Old Kingdom tombs of Dynasty 1 at Abydos.
See Green for other examples of this type (1989:269).

# Papyrus & the *Book of the Dead*

The tall papyrus plant (*Cyperus papyrus*) grew in abundance in marshes along the banks of the Nile and was the primary plant for making paper in ancient Egypt. To make the paper, the stem of the plant was first cut into lengths about a foot long. The outer coating was peeled and the interior, having a texture similar to celery, was sliced into long thin strips about half an inch wide. These strips were laid flat, one set vertically and one set horizontally on top of the first. When the strips were pressed together under a weight, the water was expressed, and the plant's own starch functioned as an adhesive binder (British Museum 1975:80). When more than one page was needed for a longer document, individual sheets were glued together to make a roll, the longest known measuring 135 feet.

### The *Book of the Dead*

The most ubiquitous use of papyrus was as a medium for funerary manuscripts of the *Book of the Dead*, which were written as instructions to enable the spirit of the deceased to travel safely from this world to the next. The manuscripts, which were placed in the burial chamber with the deceased, contained spells, incantations, and prayers. The text was written in hieroglyphs or in one of the cursive scripts, either hieratic or demotic; vignettes or illuminations relating to certain spells were often painted on the papyrus (British Museum 1975:76, 77, 81).

The practice of placing the *Book of the Dead* in the burial chamber began in Dynasty 18 and continued into the Ptolemaic Period. In the Old Kingdom, similar texts, called *Pyramid Texts*, were inscribed on the walls of the burial chamber, and in the Middle Kingdom *Coffin Texts* were inscribed on sarcophagi. The *Book of the Dead* evolved from these earlier texts (British Museum 1975:157–9).

*Continued on page 16.*

**16**
**Papyrus manuscript**
Ptolemaic Period (304–30 BC)
Papyrus, pigment
L: 12.5 in. (31.8 cm), W: 11 in. (28 cm) (as shown)
Smith collection: *David Aug '48 125.–*
E.S. David was a Long Island antiquities dealer of Middle Eastern descent who was active in the 1930s–1950s.

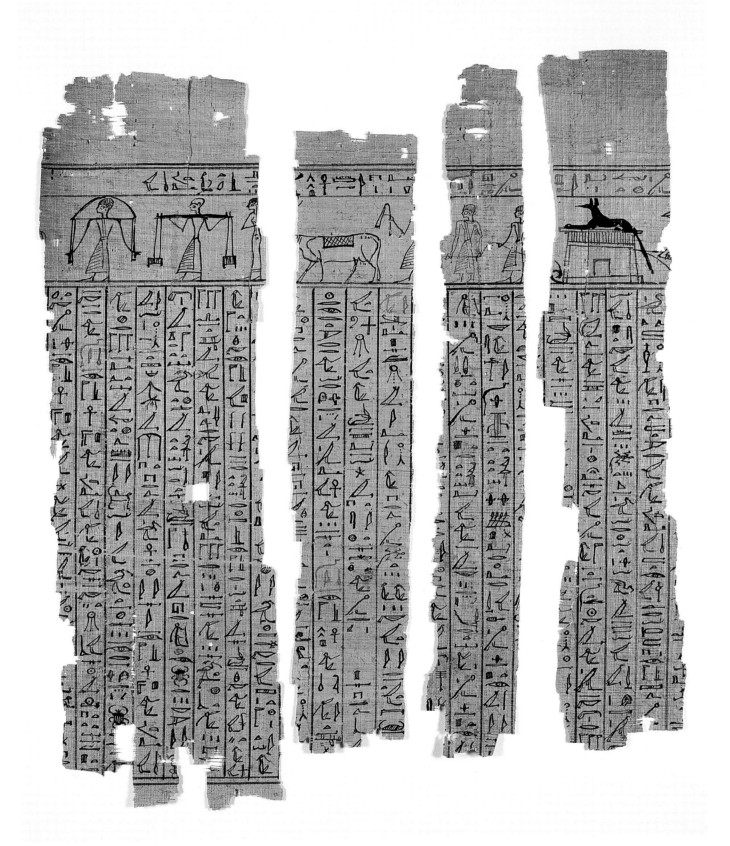

The name of the owner of the present papyrus was Ankh-Hap, *He lives for Apis*, a name common in the Late and Ptolemaic Periods (Ranke 1935:65.25). It is not possible to pinpoint the individual, as the names of his parents are not given in this portion and there are several Ankh-Haps in historical record. Ankh-Hap's title is given above in the vignette: [...] *in the temple of Amen.*

The papyrus shown here contains portions of Chapter One, Two, Three, and Eight of the *Book of the Dead*, as well as another undetermined text fragment. The vignette across the top of the scroll shows a funerary procession; vignettes such as this one customarily accompany Chapters One through Eight. An ox is depicted in the act of pulling the funerary barque, only the lotiform prow of which is visible to the right of the Anubis shrine; attendants are also depicted in the cortege, possibly carrying a set of scales for weighing the heart of the deceased, a procedure discussed on page 34.

As there are evidently some losses and as no two texts of the *Book of the Dead* are exactly alike in terms of the content, spells, and incantations, it is difficult to determine just how much may be lacking in the present example. However, the segments have been ordered in their proper sequence.

A related papyrus in the Oriental Institute (Milbank 10486), dating to the Ptolemaic Period, shows a similar funerary cortege in the first portion of the scroll, including Chapters One through Eight (Allen 1960:pl.52). Like the present example, Milbank 10486 is written in black ink, with red rubrication for whole spells, titles, introductory words, et cetera; the texts of both papyri may be correlated. Interestingly, both examples exhibit a comparatively rare feature of having the figures of the hieroglyphic text and those of the vignette facing in opposite directions. Another papyrus which exhibits this feature is a text and upper register vignette that describes the ritual of embalming in the Louvre (AE/N 5158) (cf. Boulanger 1982:293).

The partial but sequential translation of the text represented here is ordered according to similar, corresponding, documented translations of Chapters in Allen's comprehensive translation of the *Book of the Dead* (1974:5–10). It reads from right to left:

Lines 1–5 correspond with *Book of the Dead* Ch. 1, of the spell proper, sections 5–6

(5) *He enters praised and goes forth loved. He triumphs; his command is executed in the house of Osiris. He goes that he may speak with you.*

(6) *You detest me by many mouths. My soul has been confronted with my heart and it has found that I was discreet on earth. I am before you O lord of the gods. I have reached the pool of two truths, appearing as a living god and shining as the [Ennead]. I exist like one of you [...]*

Lines 6–8 correspond with *Book of the Dead* Ch. 1, of the spell proper, section 7

*Hail to you Foremost of the Westerners, who resides in...*

*...May I proceed in peace to the West. [They] make room for me beside the elders in the council in peace to the west. [...]*

*The lords of the sacred land [receive] me in peace*

Lines 9–10 and a portion of 15 correspond with *Book of the Dead* Ch. 2, of the spell proper, sections 1–2

(1) *O sole one who shines as the moon, may[the deceased] go forth amid this your multitude. Savior of those who are in the Sunshine, open not for him the nether world.*

(2) *[the deceased] is gone forth by day to do whatever he may wish on earth among the living.*

Lines 11–12 correspond with *Book of the Dead* Ch. 3, rubric and spell proper, section 1

*Recitation by the Osiris Ankh-Hap:*

*O! Atum, Atum who came forth as the Great One from the Surging flood, blessed one, even Ruty, would that you would speak to the ancestors...*

Lines 13–14 correspond with  Book of the Dead Ch. 8, spells proper (a) and (b)

(8a) *[My seal is upon Thoth who transfigured the eye of Horus.]*

*blessed one, ornament in the pate of Re the father of the gods.*

(8b) *This is I, Osiris, the lord of the West. Osiris knows the whole spell. I exist yonder, I am Suty who is with the gods. I shall not perish. Stand Horus, that he may count you among the gods.*

Lines 15–20 continue with portions from other Chapters from the *Book of the Dead*.

**17**
**Scribe's brush pot**
Dynasty 19 (1303–1200 BC)
Faience★
H: 1.75 in. (4.4 cm), D: 1.3125 in. (3.3 cm)
Smith collection: *From Buckle collection found at Memphis in 1862.*
*Used in temples about the time of Moses. Bot of Dr. Banks, no. 116,*
*Jan. 29, 1940 (8.–) Collection of 14 175.–*

In an era when few people were literate and the written word
had the potential for religious significance, the scribe was an
especially important individual. The scribe carried a kit that
included a pen or brush holder, ink palette, and brush washer
or water pot, like the present example. This kit is depicted in
the *sesh* hieroglyph, with the parts connected by a cord.
For a complete scribe's writing kit from the collection of the
Oriental Institute in Chicago, see *National Geographic* (1978: 143).
Examples of writing on papyrus, shabtys, and other objects,
are shown throughout this catalogue.

★Throughout this catalogue, the term faience is used to describe a glazed
or self-glazing composition made of a sandy core with a binder.

# THE SARCOPHAGUS

**18**
**Sarcophagus panel**
Late Period (760–330 BC)
Cartonnage, wood, pigment
L: 10.25 in. (26 cm), W: 8 in. (20.3 cm)
Ex collection Edward Budde, New York

The composition of this panel includes an ornamental frieze with stylized uræus designs along the top, two lateral sections of inscription, and two central panels with mummiform depictions of two of the Four Sons of Horus: the falcon-headed Qebsennuef and jackal-headed Duamutef, with inscriptions identifying each. The gods wear wigs and their bodies are wrapped with blue and red striped bands, the ends of which are trailing from their waists. See page 37 for a description of the uræus.

As the guardians of the deceased's organs, the Four Sons of Horus were often depicted or addressed in hieroglyphic spells in tomb paintings and, as in the present example, on panels of the sarcophagus. On the right and left of the panel, columns of inscription repeat spells to Hapi, another of the Four Sons, and Duamutef. Placement of these column texts is unrelated to the visual depictions of the deities; the Hapi text is placed next to the image of Duamutef and the Duamutef text next to the image of Qebsennuef. See page 38 for an amulet of Qebsennuef and for futher discussion of the Four Sons.

The inscriptions on this panel relate the deceased to the deities with three appositive phrases: *the venerated one*, *your son*, and *True of Voice*. Unfortunately, the actual name of the deceased is not present.

Translation:
Right side: *The venerated one before Hapi your son whom you love, True of Voice*
Left side: *The venerated one before Duamutef your son whom you love, True of Voice*

**19**

**Face from a sarcophagus**
Third Intermediate Period (1085–715 BC)
Wood (probably *acacia*), gesso, pigment
L: 10.75 in. (27.3 cm), W: 10.5 in. (26.7 cm)
Ex collection Charles Dikran Kelekian
The Kelekians were an Armenian family who were well
established in the Parisian antiquities trade in the 1920s.
Charles Dikran Kelekian came to New York shortly after
World War II and established his own business in Manhattan,
where he became a well-respected antiquarian and dealer.
The present object was acquired about 1974 from Kelekian's
shop where, according to the purchaser, its presence had been
noted for some years previously (Taylor: 1997).

Wooden anthropoid coffins depicting images of the deceased were
first used in the Middle Kingdom (Lacovara in D'Auria 1988: 105)
and, with some variations on the type, continued to be used
through the Third Intermediate or Saite Period (Dynasty 26)
(Haynes in Ibid.: 163–4). The present example, with details carved
in relief, probably dates to the Third Intermediate Period. In the
Late Period, anthropoid coffins were more simply shaped and
details were painted on their surfaces, not carved. At this time,
one-piece anthropoid cartonnage cases were made by forming
them around the mummy bundle (see cat. 20). Later, in the Roman
Period, visual identities were rendered even more cursorily; a flat
board painted with a portrait was simply incorporated into the
facial area of mummy bundle to immortalize the likeness of the
deceased.

This coffin mask is a sensitively rendered, though stylized,
portrait face, probably of a woman. It was separately carved and
then pegged to the lid of the sarcophagus. The once fully-painted
surface retains traces of the original black and white pigment and
gesso around the inner orbital planes, nose, and chin. Truncated
ends of the attachment pegs are visible on the back of the mask.

**20**

**Fragment of a sarcophagus**
Late Period (760–330 BC)
Cartonnage, pigment
L: 5.5 in. (14 cm), W: 4 in. (10.2 cm)
From an old New England collection

This fragment, most likely from the foot of a sarcophagus, depicts
an image of Anubis and a pair of horns that probably represent Isis.
Though wood was the preferred material for coffin construction,
cartonnage, made of gummed linen and plaster, was developed as
an inexpensive substitute. In the Ptolemaic Period, discarded
papyrus documents were used in place of cloth to create an even
more affordable version (Taylor in D'Auria 1988: 166). See page 38
for a description of Anubis.

**21**

**Head**

New Kingdom (1558–1085 BC)

Stone

L: 1.125 in. (2.9 cm)

Smith collection

This portrait head with sensitively modeled features, prominent, delicate eyes, a gently smiling mouth, full lips, and strong chin, is a fragment from a small statue of a nobleman or ruler. The subject wears a double or duplex wig, which was fashionable during the New Kingdom. Its popularity continued from the reign of Amenhotep III into the Ramesside Period (cf. Fay in Brovarski 1982:175, cat.198). The upper portion of this wig was composed of crimped locks of hair and the lower portion, consisting of tightly twisted curls, was draped forward over the shoulders, as can be seen on the present example.

**22**

**Figure of a kneeling rower**

First Intermediate Period–early Middle Kingdom

(circa 2160–1991 BC)

Wood, pigment

H: 7.875 in. (20 cm)

Condition: one foot missing

Smith collection: *From Count Colona Walewski Collection, Bot of Bodley Jan. 13, 1941 18.–*

Count Alexandre Florian Joseph Colonna Walewski (1810–1868) was the illegitimate son of Polish countess Francoise de Bernardy and Napoleon Bonaparte, whose exploits in Egypt initiated Europe's collection and study of Egyptian civilization in the modern era. Count Walewski, as stipulated in Bonaparte's will, labored in the diplomatic service of France, most notably under Napoleon III; however, there is no indication that he visited Egypt (de Bernardy 1957:*passim*).

*See page 24 for description.*

# SERVANT FIGURES

Servant figures, which were placed in tombs of noble
Egyptians, were intended to transcend death with the
deceased and continue their work in the next world.
They depicted the scope of domestic life of the era, and
were three-dimensional representations of scenes and
activities also shown in painting and relief sculpture on
tomb walls.

The first crudely-made Egyptian human statues in clay
and ivory, probably intended as servant statues, have been
found in pre-historic burials from before 3100 BC. During
Dynasty 4, such depictions were replaced entirely by limestone statuary of servants engaged in daily tasks. These
figures principally occurred in non-royal tombs in the
cemeteries of Giza and Sakkara, but by the end of the
Dynasty 6, servant figures of carved wood predominated
in cemeteries throughout an even wider area. At this time,
several figures were often joined to a single plank or base,
illustrating different tasks related to the same industry or
occupation.

The early Middle Kingdom marked the florescence of free-
standing groups of wooden figures in Middle and Upper
Egypt. Whereas earlier subjects tended to be concerned
almost entirely with food preparation, during this period a
broader subject matter, which represented the entire house-
hold of the tomb owner including agriculture, fishing, and
other trades, was represented. The largest known deposit
of these figures is from the tomb of Djhuty-Nakht from
Bersheh, now housed jointly in the Museum of Fine Arts
in Boston and the Cairo Museum; it includes fifty-five boats
with their crew, at least thirty-three workshops, and a dozen
or more individual figures carrying offerings. Because the
present examples carry no particular attributes, it is difficult
to determine precisely to what kind of model they belonged,
but it is likely that cat.22, because of its kneeling position,
was an oarsman (cf. Breasted 1948:pl.64, 72, 73 for similar
examples).

Very few carved wooden servant figures have been found
from later than the second half of Dynasty 12. At this time,
shabty figures, especially those bearing lengthy inscriptions,
began to appear in significant quantities. These abbreviated
mummiform figures supplanted the more humanistic occu-
pational wooden sculptures as companions of the dead. See
D'Auria (1988:p.113–15, fig. 59–69) for examples of
various model scenes with figures.

**23**
**Standing figure from a model**
First Intermediate Period – early Middle Kingdom
(circa 2160–1991 BC)
Wood, pigment
H: 9.25 in. (23.5 cm)
Ex Cairo Museum
Paper label: *Boatman from Funery* (sic) *Bark. Cairo Museum.*
*1906. C.M.L.*

# SHABTYS

Shabtys* are mummiform servant figures that were first made in Dynasty 11 of wax, clay, or wood; later, faience and stone were also employed. The early single figures were sometimes inscribed with the name of the deceased and were probably intended to symbolize the tomb owner. From the start of Dynasty 12, shabtys were inscribed with text from Chapter Six of the *Book of the Dead*. A passage from this chapter described the shabty's responsibilities: it was to do all the work of the deceased in the afterworld, especially cultivation, irrigation, and carrying burdens:

> *Spell for making an ushabti work (for a man) in god's domain.*
>
> *To be said by N. [name of the deceased]* :
>
> *O thou ushabti, if Osiris N. is counted off to do any work that is wont to be done yonder in god's domain – lo, obstacles have been set up for him yonder – (as) a man to his duties,*
>
> *thou art charged with all (these (tasks) that are wont to be done yonder), to cultivate the fields, to irrigate the shores, to transport sand of the west or of the east. "I will do (them); here I am," shalt thou say* (Allen 1974:8).

The shabty carried various agricultural implements that were instrumental to its tasks: both a narrow and a broad bladed hoe, baskets, bags, moulds for brick making, whips, and pots for carrying. The bags and baskets were empty and the tools were held in readiness to begin. The earliest shabtys were accompanied by separate molded implements, but later these attributes were painted on or shaped in relief.

In Dynasty 25 and early Dynasty 26, a new arrangement of tools for the shabty evolved, consisting of a pick and hoe and small seed bag suspended from a cord slung over the left shoulder. During this phase, shabtys were customarily made of faience with a distinctive pale green or blue-green glaze.

The number of shabtys made for the deceased varied and likely depended on the economic status of the owner. During the late Middle Kingdom and early New Kingdom, the number of shabtys for private individuals usually did not exceed five, and in early Dynasty 19, ten. Towards the end of Dynasty 18, royal shabtys numbered 365, one for every day in the year, and one overseer for every ten figures, equaling 401 shabtys. However, a wide variety of numbers might be found; Tutankhamun's tomb, for instance, contained 417 shabtys.

---

* Slight variations of the term occurred throughout history, including shabti, shawabty, and ushabti.

## 24
## Shabty of Ta-Rekhet
Dynasty 19 (1303–1200 BC)
Wood, pigment
L: 8 in. (20.3 cm)
Smith collection: *Bot of Dr. Banks, no. 5, Mar. 22, 1940 (50.–) Collection of 10 175.–*

---

This female wooden shabty belonged to the *Lady of the House* named Ta-Rekhet, meaning *Wise One* or *Knowing One*. Ta-Rekhet was a known female name in the New Kingdom (Ranke 1935:365.5). Her detailed painting includes coiffeur, jewelry, and garments, which are representative of New Kingdom style. She wears a long dark blue, tripartite wig, a multi-stranded *wesekh* collar of red and black which extends downward and over her crossed arms, and a bracelet with six vertical rows of beads in red.

To accomplish her labors in the next world, this shabty grasps a hoe in each hand. On her back she carries a yoke with two water pots and a large rectangular basket with red woven fibers. According to Schneider, water pots and yoke were depicted first on shabty in late Dynasty 18 (1977, vol.I:170).

There are five horizontal rows of text on the front and one vertical column up the back of this figure. As is typical for the Ramesside period (Dynasties 19–20), the hieroglyphs were painted in black with a yellow background and separating lines in red. For other polychrome wooden shabtys of this period, see Reeves (1984:40, pl.32b), Petrie (1914b:165, pl.xxxiii), Schneider (1977, vol.III: pl.16, pl.11 #3.1.1.20), Chappaz (1984:23, #003), and Reeves (in D'Auria 1988:155, cat.104).

**25**
**Shabty**
Dynasties 18–19 (1558–1200 BC)
Alabaster
H: 8 in. (20.3 cm)
Excavated by W.M.F. Petrie at Gurob; Smith collection:
*From the Price Coll. April 17, 1942 Bodley 35.–*
(see frontispiece for front view in color)

Shabtys were made of alabaster only in late Dynasty 18 and through Dynasty 19, making them relatively rare. This translucent alabaster shabty, wearing a wig and standing solemnly with its arms folded, has finely detailed and serene facial features. The relatively simple features and lack of implements are consistent with its dating to late Dynasty 18 or early Dynasty 19. See Reeves (1984: IV, pl. 34 a, b) and Schneider (1977, vol. III: pl. 29, 3.2.4.10, 3.2.4.11) for similar Dynasty 18 shabtys, and see Schneider (1977, vol. III: 3.2.1.20, 3.2.1.26, 3.2.1.36) for examples from early Dynasty 19.

The present example was excavated by Petrie at Gurob (Hilton Price 1897: 163), a site which, according to Petrie, was occupied for less than a century: "its history covers the end of the XVIIIth dynasty and the beginning of the XIXth" (1890: 32). The figure was subsequently acquired by Frederick George Hilton Price, a British banker and inveterate collector of antiquities. He published this shabty in a luxurious two-volume work of his large collection of Egyptian art (1897: 163). In the introduction to his catalogue, Hilton Price described his solid collection:

> With the view of making my collection of Egyptian antiquities,
> which comprises over 4,000 objects, more useful to those who take
> an intelligent interest in such things, I have prepared the Cata-
> logue of it which is printed in the following pages, but I warn
> the reader at once that it contains neither large stone objects,
> nor mummies, nor objects the natural place of which is a public
> museum (1897: iv).

In 1911, the present object was sold with the rest of the Hilton Price collection by the London auctioneers Sotheby, Wilkinson & Hodge (Sotheby, Wilkinson & Hodge 1911: 141, lot 1136, pl. XXV). Its whereabouts from that time until it was acquired by Bodley, and finally sold to Smith in 1942, have not been established.

Notations written on the object on its 19th century marble base are evidence of its interesting collection history. Lettered in ink on the foot of the figure is *XIX Dyn. Gurob* and *530*; marked in ink on the bottom of the stand are the numbers *1575* and *433*, and in pencil the number *2* and *Price Sale*. "1575" was the number given to the object by Hilton Price, "2" refers to the fact that in the Sotheby's "Price Sale," there were two shabtys in the lot, and "433" is the accession number given to the object by the Endowment for Biblical Research.

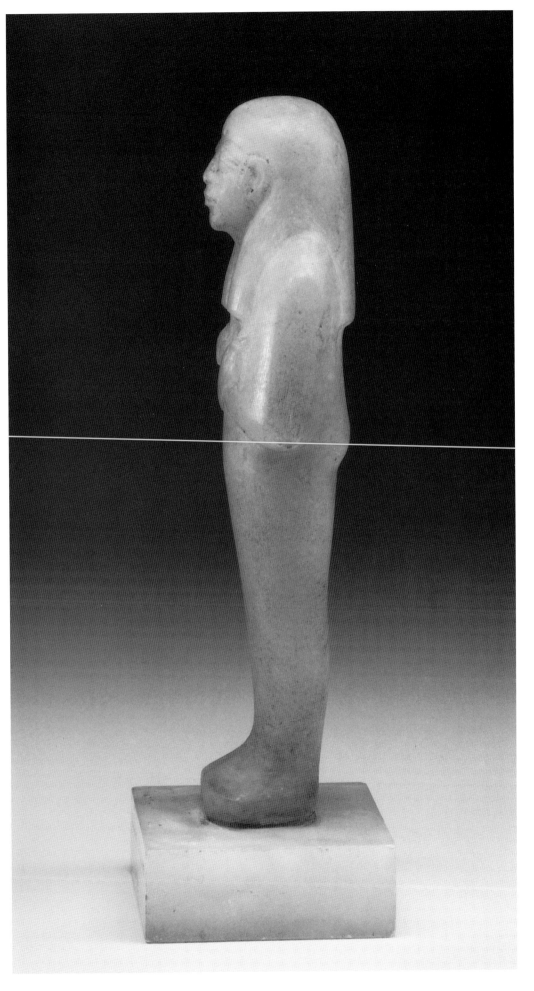

**26**
**Shabty of Pa-di-Ptah**
Dynasties 25–26 (760–525 BC)
Faience, pigment
L: 2.875 in. (7.3 cm)
Smith collection: *From Buckle collection, Bot of Dr. Banks, no. 25, Aug. 27, 1937  25.–*

This shabty has single line of horizontal inscription below the folded arms and a single line of vertical inscription on the lower portion of the body; his hair, beard, and the inscription have been painted in black. The figure is inscribed with the name and title of the owner; his name is Pa-di-Ptah, meaning *The gift of Ptah*, and his title is divine father of Bastet. Bastet's title is also inscribed: *Mistress of Life of the Two Lands,* which are Upper and Lower Egypt.

Pa-di-Ptah lived in late Dynasty 25 or early Dynasty 26, in Memphis. The fact that the Buckle collection was assembled largely from objects collected in Memphis in 1862 is consistent with this inscription, which associates Pa-di-Ptah firmly with that city. Shabtys of this period carry two hoes and no seed bag; the pillar on the back of the figure forms a continuous plane with the base.

Other shabtys of Pa-di-Ptah are known in museum collections in Berlin, Brussels, Cairo, Copenhagen, Leningrad, London, Marseilles, and Strasbourg (cf. Aubert 1974:216–7, pl.55, fig.133)

**27**
**Shabty**
Dynasties 27–30 (525–341 BC)
Faience
L: 4 in. (10.2 cm)
Ex Burton Holmes collection;
Smith collection: *Bodley, Dec. 26 1940*
Burton Holmes (1870–1958) was a traveler, photographer, and the author of the travelogue *The World is Mine* (1953).

**28**
**Shabty**
Dynasties 27–30 (525–341 BC)
Faience
L: 3.375 in. (8.6 cm)
Smith collection

**29**
**Shabty**
New Kingdom, possibly Dynasty 18 (1558–1303 BC)
Stone, pigment
L: 4.375 in. (11.1 cm)
With a mid-19th century paper label glued to the front of the body, the text of which is reproduced on an accompanying tag, circa 1900: *Stone model of a mummy found in a tomb in Egypt, probably as old as the time of Moses*

This shabty of porous stone has remains of black painted details, including a diadem and basket on the back, and on the front, traces of facial detail, wig, and a single line of inscription, which is obscured by the paper label.

**30**
**Shabty of Rameses-Nakht**
Dynasties 19–20 (1303–1085 BC)
Faience
L: 5.5 in. (14 cm)
Condition: rejoined, feet restored
Ex collection Theodore W. and Frances S. Robinson
During the 1920s Theodore W. and Frances S. Robinson assembled a large collection of antiquities. The majority of their collection was a superb selection of ancient glass, which they donated to the Art Institute of Chicago in the 1940s (Alexander 1994:12-13); a smaller group of objects, including the present example, descended in the Robinson family.

This cream glazed shabty with brown details belonged to a man named Rameses-Nakht, *Rameses is strong*; his title *general...leader of the troops* is written on the front of the body in a single line of hieroglyphs. A well known tomb owner, named Rameses-Nakht lived in the time of Rameses X in Dynasty 20.

**31**
**Shabty of Pa-Sen**
Dynasty 21 (1085–945 BC)
Faience
L: 4 in. (10.2 cm)
Condition: rejoined
Ex collection Arnold Coward
Coward, a survivor of Nazi torture, founded a small private museum in Honolulu to exhibit an eclectic assemblage of artifacts, including torture devices, *memento mori*, and a number of significant Egyptian pieces.

This figure, with bright blue glaze and black painted details, and a single vertical line of inscription, is typical of Dynasty 21 shabtys. The figure holds a single implement, which is either a hoe or a whip; the presence of a whip could indicate that this is an overseer figure.

This is a shabty of a man named Pa-sen, *The Brother*, whose priestly title is *God's Father of Amen* (Ranke 1935:117.6). This priestly title is found on a number of shabtys in Leiden that are all of Deir El Bahri Cache from Dynasty 21 (Schneider 1977: cat. 4.3.1.52, 53, 64, 65).

**32**
**Shabty of Horemheb**
Dynasty 30–Ptolemaic Period (378–30 BC)
Faience
L: 6.25 in. (15.9 cm)
Smith collection: *From Buckle collection, Bot of Dr. Banks,*
*Aug. 1937 45.–*

This excellent example of a pale green glazed shabty has ten horizontal lines of inscription on the lower portion of the body. Finely
detailed implements, including hoe blade, seed bag, and flail are
carefully rendered. The figure's owner was Horemheb, *Horus is in*
*festival*, whose mother was Takhawti. See Newberry (1957:253,
no.47859) for other examples of shabtys of this individual.

**33**
**Shabty of Imhotep**
Dynasties 27–30 (525–341 BC)
Faience
L: 7.5 in. (19.1 cm)
Smith collection: *Bot of Morgan, the dragoman* [translator and guide]
*on the Nile in 1938 15.–*

This shabty has ten lines of horizontal inscription. The owner
of the figure was Imhotep. He was named after the architect of the
Step Pyramid of Dynasty 3, who was venerated in the Late Period.
The name was subsequently given to many male children.

## 34
**Heart scarab**

New Kingdom (1558–1085 BC)
Probably green jasper (*nmhf*)
L: 2.5 in. (6.4 cm), W: 1.75 in. (4.4 cm)
Ex collection William Tilden Blodgett (1823–1875)
A co–founder, generous patron, and chairman of the first executive committee of the Metropolitan Museum of Art in the 1870s, William Tilden Blodgett was a capitalist who made his fortune in the varnish business and in real estate investments. He was also a liberal-minded reformer, a leading abolitionist, and a founder of *The Nation* magazine. Blodgett had a substantial personal art collection (Tomkins 1970:31–46); during the last years of his life, he resided in Europe where he purchased three important collections of 17th century "Old Master" paintings, which became the nucleus of the Metropolitan Museum's collection. An avid traveler and collector, he visited Egypt in the 1870s (Tyng 1875:42).

The ancient Egyptians believed the heart to be the seat of judgement and intelligence. Vital to rebirth and afterlife, it was not removed from the embalmed body as other organs were. At the final judgement, the deceased's heart would be weighed against an ostrich feather, symbol of the goddess Maat, or against the goddess herself. The heart might bear witness against its owner, but if the weighing was successful and the heart was judged virtuous, the deceased would be allowed to enter the heavenly kingdom of Osiris, the land of eternal life.

Amulets of the scarab (*Scarabaeus sacer*), or dung beetle, were popular as a symbol of regeneration and new life; since scarab eggs are laid in, and the young hatched from, a ball of dung, it was believed that the beetle had the power of spontaneous generation (Andrews 1994:50). During the New Kingdom, a "heart" scarab, like the present example, was placed over the heart on the body of the deceased (Ben Tor 1989:18); it was inscribed with spells and entreaties from Chapter Thirty of the *Book of the Dead* and the owner's name. Such inscriptions insured that the heart would not say anything which might jeopardize the eternal life of its owner by making accusations of either a true or false nature (Lurker 1986:61).

According to Petrie, the text typically inscribed on the heart scarab differs slightly from manuscript versions of Chapter Thirty in the *Book of the Dead* (1914a:24). His version follows:

> *My heart of my mother, my heart of my mother, my heart of my becoming (in future life). May nothing rise up against me in evidence; may no hindrance be made against me by the divine chiefs; may there be no enemy of thee against me in the presence of the Guardian of the Balance. Thou art my ka in my body, the creator making sound my limbs. Come forth to the bliss towards which we are bound. May our name not be in bad odor with the Ministrants, those who deal to men their course in life; and be there good for us, be there good to the hearer, be there joy of heart, by the Weighing of words. May not lies be uttered in the presence of the God before the great God lord of Amenti. Behold thy uplifting is in the acquittal* (Ibid.).

Many scarabs were inscribed with only certain portions of the spell and many inscriptions contain spelling or grammatical errors, indicating that the text may not always have been fully understood by the engraver or patron (Haynes 1996). The present example is inscribed for a man named Semen-tawy and engraved with a ten-line variant of the spell (compare the scarab of Semen-tawy in Ben Tor 1989:52, no.3):

1. [...]*Semen-tawy, True of Voice, Lord of Veneration.*
2. *He says:O heart of my mother! O heart of my mother! O my heart*
3. *of my coming into being! Do not stand against me as a witness.*
4. *Do not contradict me with the judges. Do not act*
5. *as my enemy in the presence of the guardian of the balance. You are my soul*
6. *Which is in my body, which unites and makes whole*
7. *my limbs. When you go forth to that happy place transport us there.*
8. *Do not cause my name to stink in the entourage*
9. *of the one who created mankind in attendence*
10. *May it be well on earth and be well for the Hearer.*

The present example is probably composed of green jasper or *nmhf*, the stone from which the heart scarab was supposed to be carved, as prescribed by Chapter Thirty (Roth in D'Auria 1988:223). Although Petrie lists sixteen different materials and a wide variety of colors for heart scarabs (1914a:24), green jasper was especially valued for its durability and for the association of green with vegetation, regeneration, and hence immortality. The style of carving of the present example is exceptional, with a well delineated wing case, prothorax, and elytra, and carefully detailed legs and naturalistic clypeus (compare Petrie 1914a:pl. VIII, IX and D'Auria 1988:224, fig.176a, b). See Andrews for a more complete discussion of the scarab (1994:50–9).

# AMULETS

From Pre-Dynastic times until the Roman Period, ancient Egyptians adorned themselves and their dead with amulets of a wide variety of subjects and materials. These amulets were believed to give the wearer special protection, power, or ability.

In the Old Kingdom amulets took only a few forms, but by the First Intermediate Period, the occurrence of amulets increased greatly in numbers and expanded their range of types (Andrews 1994:11). One of the most important forms represented the gods and goddesses (cats.41–47). Attributes of these gods and their animal incarnations (cats.35–6, 39–40) or talismans were also popular, and by the Late Period the repertoire of subjects had increased to several hundred. Another group of amulets represented food, clothing, or other possessions that might be useful to the deceased in the afterlife (cat.38). These images were incorporated into funeral accoutrements, and were wrapped within or depicted upon the linen bandages surrounding the mummy, or used for other adornments for the corpse. For a complete discussion of amulets and their meanings, see Andrews (1994), Reisner (1907), and Petrie (1914a).

The Egyptian amulet and jewelry maker used a variety of semi-precious stones, minerals, and human-made materials; during the New Kingdom and Late Period, the use of faience predominated. Faience was popular because it could be molded to virtually any shape. The blue-green color of most faience glazes was probably intended to imitate turquoise, a stone precious to the ancient Egyptians. The range of colors from light green to blue-green was associated with rebirth and regeneration, and were thus a very popular color for amulets, the majority of whose function or reference had to do not only with protection, but also the enabling of rebirth, rejuvenation, and the quest for immortality.

**35**
**Sow amulet**
Third Intermediate Period (1085–715 BC) or later
Faience
L: 1.25 in. (3.2 cm)
Smith collection: *From Buckle collection, Bot of Dr. Banks, no. 165, Sept. 20, 1937 6.–*

**36**
**Sow amulet**
Third Intermediate Period (1085–715 BC) or later
Faience
L: 1.125 in. (2.9 cm)
Smith collection: *From Buckle collection, Bot of Dr. Banks, no. 239, Aug. 27, 1937 6.–*

The large sow represents Nut, the goddess of the sky. The heavenly bodies were Nut's children, who "enter her mouth and emerge again from her womb" (Lurker 1986:90). The sow was likened to this goddess because she was known to have a habit of eating her own piglets. These amulets first appeared in Third Intermediate Period burials, and were intended to represent divine motherhood and give the wearer fertility.

**37**
**Uræus amulet**
Dynasty 26 (664–525 BC) or later
Faience
L: 0.9375 in. (2.4 cm)
Smith collection: *From Buckle collection, Bot from Dr. Banks, no. 224, Sept. 1937 6.–*

The uræus, or rearing cobra, was a royal insignia worn on the forehead, primarily by Horus and Seth, and probably represented the goddess Hathor (Luker 1986: 125). Royal symbols such as this were often worn by non-royal people, signifying a wish for elevated status. Because the cobra sheds its skin, it also signified the power of rebirth and regeneration. Uræus amulets were relatively common in Dynasty 26 and later. See also cat.60 for a bronze uræus.

**38**
**Duck amulet**
New Kingdom (1558–1085 BC)
Faience
L: 1 in. (2.5 cm)
Smith collection: *From Buckle collection, Bot of Dr. Banks, no. 443, Sept. 20, 1937 3.–*

The bright-blue color and the flat one-sided shape of this duck are typical of New Kingdom style.

**39**
**Ibis amulet**
Third Intermediate Period–Late Period (1085–330 BC)
Faience
L: 1.1875 in. (3 cm)
Smith collection: *From Buckle collection, Bot of Dr. Banks, no. 234, Sept. 20, 1937 5.–*

**40**
**Ibis amulet**
Dynasty 26 (664–525 BC)
Faience
L: 1.5 in. (3.8 cm)
From an old New England collection

Ibis amulets, first found in First Intermediate Period burials, represented Thoth, the god of wisdom and writing; he was the divine scribe and recorded the weighing of the heart in the underworld. The god was primarily depicted with the head of an ibis and a human body. Complete faience amulets representing Thoth, like the present examples, are found in the Third Intermediate Period, and last until the end of the Dynastic period. These examples are depicted with their beaks resting on a feather, the symbol of the goddess Maat, which was counter-weighed against the heart of the deceased in the ritual of judgement (see page 34 for a description of this ritual).

**41**

**Anubis amulet**
Probably Dynasty 26 (664–525 BC) or later
Faience
L: 1.4375 in. (3.7 cm)
Smith collection: *From Buckle collection, Bot of Dr. Banks,*
*no. 205, Aug. 27, 1937  5.–*

Anubis, the jackel-headed god, had numerous associations, including god of the underworld and guardian of the dead; he was the embalmers' deity. One of his most important functions in the Netherworld was to perform the ritual weighing of the heart of the deceased before Osiris and the forty-two assessor gods (Lurker 1986:28). See page 34 for a discussion of this ritual.

The image of Anubis often appeared on the doors of tombs, in depictions of funerary processions on coffins, on tomb wall paintings, and in other funerary contexts. For a depiction of Anubis on a papyrus vignette as a part of the funerary cortege, see cat. 16, for a votive bronze figure of Anubis, see cat. 54, and for a depiction of Anubis on a mummy case, see cat. 20.

**42**

**Lion-headed deity amulet**
Dynasties 21–26 (1085–525 BC)
Faience
L: 2.375 in. (6 cm)
Smith collection: *Bot of Dr. Banks, no. 244, Nov. 21, 1939 11.66*

This striding lion-headed goddess is a combination of the Theban goddess Mut and the lion-headed Sekhmet. The double crown she wears was customarily sacred to the goddess Mut, consort of Amen-Re of Thebes (Andrews 1994: 22, 34).

**43**

**Bastet amulet**
Dynasties 21–26 (1085–525 BC)
Faience
L: 0.75 in. (1.9 cm)
Smith collection: *From Buckle collection, Bot of Dr. Banks, no. 174,*
*Sept. 20, 1937  3.–*

This finely-featured cat-headed goddess, seated on a low throne, represents Bastet. The long, pointed ears distinguish her from the round-eared lion-headed goddess, Sekhmet. See page 48 for a description of these two feline goddesses and their various attributes (Andrews 1994: 32–3).

**44**

**Taweret amulet**
Dynasties 21–26 (1085–525 BC)
Faience
L: 1.625 in. (4.1 cm)
Smith collection: *From Buckle collection, Bot of Dr. Banks, no. 173,*
*Sept. 20, 1937  4.–*

Taweret, meaning *The Great One*, is the pregnant hippopotamus goddess with pendulous breasts and a crocodile tail. She holds a *sa* sign, meaning protection, in her front feet. Taweret was especially sacred to women in childbirth; she was believed to be the spouse of Bes, also a protective deity (see page 40 for a description of Bes). This amulet is pierced through the upper back of the tail for suspension (cf. Andrews 1994: 40, fig. 39).

**45**

**Khnum amulet**
Probably Dynasty 26 (664–525 BC) or later
Faience
L: 1.5625 in. (4 cm)
Smith collection: *Bot of Dr. Banks, no. 216, Nov. 21, 1939  11.66*

Khnum, the creator god and guardian of the Nile, is represented in human form with a ram's head. His devotees believed that he created gods and humans from clay, the mud of the Nile, on a potter's wheel (Ions 1968: 38).

**46**

**Nehebkau amulet**
Dynasties 21–26 (1085–525 BC)
Faience
L: 1.625 in. (4.1 cm)
Condition: rejoined
Smith collection: *From Buckle collection, Bot of Dr. Banks, no. 171,*
*Sept. 20, 1937*

The god Nehebkau is represented with a human body and the long tail and head of a snake; in this example, he holds his human arms up, supporting his head. This god can also take the form of a coiled upright snake or snake-headed human leaning on a long snake's tail. Nehebkau symbolized power and was one of the forty-two assessor gods who judge the deceased; amulets of this god were first found in burials of the Third Intermediate Period.

**47**

**Qebsennuef amulet**
Dynasties 25–26 (760–525 BC)
Faience
L: 1.625 in. (4.1 cm)
Smith collection: *From Buckle collection, Bot of Dr. Banks, no. 474,*
*Aug. 27, 1937  5.–*

This amulet represents Qebsennuef, one of the Four Sons of Horus, who was charged with guarding the intestines of the deceased. Representations of the Four Sons are primarily seen on figural tops of canopic jars, in which the organs were stored for entombment. Each Son was associated with a specific protective goddess, and with one of the four cardinal directions; each was in charge of safeguarding a particular organ, which was removed from the body and stored in the appropriate jar when the mummy was embalmed. The human-headed Imsety, associated with Isis and the south, guarded the liver; the baboon-headed Hapi, associated with Nephthys and the north, guarded the lungs; the jackel-headed Duamutef, associated with Neith and the east, guarded the stomach; and the falcon-headed Qebsennuef, associated with Selket and the west, guarded the intestines.

In the Third Intermediate Period, when mummified organs were placed back into the body cavity, canopic jars were not required. Thereafter, flat amuletic depictions of the Four Sons in profile, usually made of pierced faience, like the present example, were probably stiched onto the cloth wrapping of the mummy. The style of this amulet, holding the very long scarf, dates from Dynasty 25 to 26.

# Bes

The long Egyptian tradition of funeral rites for immortality and the preservation of the soul of the deceased coexisted with a cadre of deities who labored for the relief of physical and psychological concerns of the living. Bes was one such deity associated with daily life; the ancient Egyptians invoked him as a guardian of the defenseless, including the sleeping, children, women in childbirth, and as a protector against the evil eye. His image often appeared on implements connected with eye cosmetics and on mirror handles (Romano 1982: 223–4, 226–7). Amulets of his visage, such as the present examples, were commonly used in daily life, primarily by women or children (Capel 1996: 73).

Bes evolved in the Middle Kingdom from representations of a lion demon who, in earlier periods, was invoked during protective rituals and impersonated by sorcerers (Bourriau 1988: 110–112). Bes' features reflect this derivation; he was often depicted with a full beard, gaping mouth, often with a protruding tongue, and prancing and distorted legs, which imitate the lion's hind quarters. In later times, he was often depicted with a feather crown, sometimes holding the *sa* symbol of protection or a sword, and wearing a token lion or panther skin. Images of protection such as this were often janiform so that they could look in both directions (cats. 50, 51). The amuletic heads of Bes occured from the Third Intermediate Period onwards (Andrews 1994: 40). The yellow highlights of cat. 50 are characteristic of faience figures from the Ptolemaic and Roman Periods.

The Ptolemaic or Roman period terra cotta vessel in the shape of a Bes head (cat. 48) exhibits the ultimate morphological refinement of the deity. The lion mask has evolved into well-defined facial features with thick arched eyebrows, broad nose, high cheeks, and curling beard. The area formerly occupied by the outstretched tongue is now occupied by a small beard. Though altered, this depiction of Bes still suggests the original aura of the protective demon.

The precise origin of Bes and the antecedent lion demon is not known, although a foreign origin has been suggested (Romano 1982: 76). Typically represented full face, the Bes image differs from that of most other Egyptian deities who were usually shown in profile. Romano suggests that the exaggerated facial features of the god may be a coded reference to a foreign genesis (Ibid.). Leclant writes that the Bes image may be "a survivor of primitive totemism…bound up with the oldest traditions of prehistory" (in Vercoutter 1967: 278).

Devotion to Bes was persistent and strong, surviving even Akhenaton's iconoclastic assault on the Egyptian pantheon in Dynasty 18 (Wilson 1956: 221). The image of Bes spread across the ancient Mediterranean world during the 7th to 4th century BC; his use has been documented in Phoenicia (Ribichini in Moscati 1988: 115), Cyprus (Karageorghis in Ibid.:161 and Moscati in Ibid.: 288–9), and Carthage (Acquaro in Ibid.:396). Bes may also be identified in the figures of Silenus and Hercules from the Graeco-Roman period (Ibid.: 212, 470, 473). Similarities are also striking between the mask of Bes and the wild hair, bulging eyes, gaping mouth, and protruding tongue of the gorgon mask, which was also used as a protective image.

Bes images are ubiquitous in the literature; for some similar examples of Bes amulets, see Petrie (1914a: pl. XXXIII, XXXIV) and Andrews (1994: 39–40).

**48**
**Vase of the head of Bes**
Roman Period (30 BC–450 AD)
Terra cotta
H: 5.125 in. (13 cm)
Smith collection: *From Buckle collection found near Memphis in 1862. Used in temples about the time of Moses. Bot of Dr. Banks, no. 123, Jan. 29, 1940 (40–) Collection of 14 175.–*

**49**
**Head of Bes**
Dynasty 26 (664–525 BC) or later
Faience
L: 2 in. (5.1 cm), W: 1.5625 in. (4 cm)
Smith collection: *Bot of Dr. Banks, no. 278, Nov. 21, 1939  11.66*

**50**
**Bes amulet**
Probably Ptolemaic–Roman Periods (304 BC–450 AD)
Faience
L: 1.375 in. (3.5 cm)
Smith collection: *Bot of Dr. Banks, no. 292, Nov. 21, 1939*

**51**
**Double-faced Bes amulet**
Probably Dynasty 26 (664–525 BC)
Faience
L: 2.1875 in. (5.6 cm)
Smith collection: *from Memphis, Buckle collection. Bot of Dr. Banks, Feb. 27, 1941 (35.–) 4 for 100.–*

**52**

**Ptahtek amulet**
Dynasty 26 (664–525 BC)
Faience
H: 3.375 in. (8.6 cm)
Smith collection: *from Memphis Buckle collection. Bot of Dr. Banks, Feb. 27, 1941 (30.–) 4 for 100.–*
(see back cover for back view)

---

Ptahtek, the muscular dwarf god, is represented here in his customary pose, standing naked with clenched hands resting on his thighs. He is characteristically bald with finely delineated facial features, hands, and toes, and carefully modelled leg muscles and buttocks. Behind the neck is a striated loop for suspension and the figure stands on a small trapezoidal base. Amuletic representations of Ptahtek were typically made of faience from the Third Intermediate Period through the Late Period; they were customarily of this large size and equipped with a suspension loop for wearing (Andrews 1994:38–9).

Although little is known of the derivation of Ptahtek, crude images appeared as early as Dynasty 6 (Andrews 1994:39). In tomb scenes of daily life, painted as early as the Old Kingdom, dwarfs were frequently depicted as workers in the precious metal workshops. This has led to speculation that the Ptahtek image may have derived from that of Ptah, the craftsman god of Memphis, who was depicted in human form with a shaven head and tightly fitting cap. Well before the end of the Old Kingdom, Ptah was worshiped as the god of creation, who, like Khnum, fashioned the other gods, men, and animals from clay on the potter's wheel (Lurker 1986:96–7).

This figure can have many names and derivations. Early writers, including Petrie, termed Ptahtek figures "Ptah-Seker" figures, associating them with the funerary Ptah-Seker-Osiris cult, which evolved in Memphis during the Late Period (Petrie 1914a:88, pl. 176). The name Pataikos was used by Herodotus for Phoenician dwarf-form gods that derived from this Egyptian prototype. For Phoenician versions of Ptahtek, see Moscati (1988:401, cat. 227, 685, 687).

Ptahtek should not be confused with the dwarf-like protective god Bes, although they do share some attributes and functions. Both are bandy legged, are often depicted brandishing snakes or weapons, and are depicted frontally. Ptahtek, however, has a more youthful demeanor and is usually depicted clean-shaven or with a single lock of hair. See the preceding pages for a discussion and examples of Bes.

# BRONZE FIGURES

Bronze casting technology was commonly used in Egypt from the Middle Kingdom onward. However, from the beginning of the Saite (664 BC) through the end of the Ptolemaic reigns (50 BC), the manufacture and use of cast bronze figures of deities was especially popular. It is believed that these figures, both solid and hollow, were made by the *cire perdue* (lost wax) technique. A skilled artist made a beeswax original, which was cast in plaster; metalworkers then mass-produced the castings. Details might be chased by hand after casting (Dunham 1937: *passim*).

Because they were produced in quantity, the cast bronze statues were affordable and popular as votive objects. Archaeological evidence indicates that such offerings were deposited in considerable numbers around temples, shrines, and other sacred sites as votive offerings and by pious Egyptians as a display of devotion to the particular deity.

The style and iconography of these works changed little during this period, making precise dating difficult. However, there was continuing diversity in quality, size, and degree of elaboration, ranging from exquisite sculptures with inlays, gilding, and personalized inscriptions, to plain, undistinguished examples. This variety may be evidence of diverse artistic talents or an indication of the budgetary requirements of consumers.

## 53
### Isis holding Horus
Third Intermediate Period–Late Period (1085–330 BC)
Bronze
H: 9.25 in. (23.5 cm)
Smith collection: *Bot of Dr. Banks Feb. 20 '39 100.*

The goddess Isis had great public appeal and was worshipped throughout Egyptian history. The image of Isis nursing her son Horus was regarded as an especially powerful and protective one. She raised Horus in seclusion in the marshes of the Delta to hide him from Seth, his wicked uncle and the murderer of his father, Osiris, the king of the Netherworld.

Isis wears a crown composed of cow horns surrounding a sun disk, attributes originally belonging to the sky goddess Hathor, mother of the sun god. During the Middle Kingdom, a close identification of Isis with Hathor led to the adoption of these attributes, which continued into Roman times.

This bronze was an *ex voto* that would have been purchased by the owner and placed in a major sanctuary or shrine. The dedication prayer is inscribed in hieroglyphs on the left side and base, and includes the owner's name: *May Isis, give life to Pa-Shed-Bastet, Son of Wedja-Hor.* Pa-Shed-Bastet, "the one that Bastet has rescued" and *Wedja-Hor,* "Sound is Horus," were both names commonly used in the Late Period (Ranke 1935: 119.15).

For a discussion of the evolution of the image of Isis, her worship in ancient Egypt, and her continuing influence on Graeco-Roman and Christian imagery and belief, see Arslan (1997: *passim*). For similar seated bronze figures of Isis and Horus, see Roeder (1950: 34, 35, 36), Pantalacci (in D'Auria 1988: 240–1), and Arslan (1997: 56–7, pl. II.19, II.22).

**54**
**Anubis**
Late Period (760–330 BC)
Bronze
L: 2.375 in. (6 cm)
Smith collection: *Bot of Morgan, dragoman* [interpreter and guide]
*on the Nile in 1938  3.75*

The striding male with a jackal head or jackal mask represents the
god Anubis. He wears a tripartite wig and short kilt, and his feet
are fixed to a thin base plate. The object in his hands is not clear,
but it is probable that it is a crook and flail, customary attributes
of this god. See Roeder (1956:58, 59, pl.9,10) for similar examples.
See page 38 for an Anubis amulet and page 20 for his image on a
fragment of a sarcophagus.

**55**
**Aegis of Isis**
Dynasty 18 (1558–1303 BC)
Bronze
L: 4 in. (10.2 cm), W: 2.375 in. (6 cm)
Smith collection: *From Vose collection, Bot of Bodley Dec. 26,*
*1940  11.25*

The Egyptian aegis was a necklace element with amuletic significance that gave the wearer protection. It was primarily worn as the
central pendant, but also sometimes as a counterpoise in the back
of the neck. Larger examples of aegises were suspended from the
prows of sacred barques. The goddesses most frequently represented on these aegises were Isis and Hathor (see page 44 for a description of these two goddesses).

Isis is shown on the present example with a tripartite wig and
uræus, and surmounted by her customary crown of sundisk and
horns. The separately-cast crown is consistent with several other
published examples, although aegises of one-part construction
were also common. For very similar bronze Isis aegises, see
Roeder (1956:469–71, pl. 64h, 65b) and Dunham (1931:104–9).
The bronze figure of a seated cat (cat.58) wears an aegis of Bastet.

**56**
**Amen**
Late Period (760–330 BC)
Bronze
L: 4 in. (10.2 cm)
Smith collection

Amen was one of the most ancient Egyptian deities, appearing early
on *Pyramid Texts* of the Old Kingdom. During the New Kingdom,
Amen, who became the god of the city of Thebes, was worshiped
as a supreme state god and merged with the sun god in the form
of Amen-Re.

This striding figure of Amen with finely rendered facial features
and delicately outlined almond-shaped eyes, is reminiscent of por-
traits of the pharaoh Amenhotep III of Dynasty 18. The pleated kilt
the figure wears is also similar to the pharaoh's traditional garment.
Pharoahs were often named after gods or incorporated the name of
gods in their own names, and likenesses of the gods made during
the pharoah's reign and thereafter were frequently modeled after
the pharoah. The identity of the god Amen is confirmed by the
fragments of his sun disc and double plume crown, traces of which
are visible along the ridge where they were attached. For another
image of Amen with the features of Amenhotep III, wearing the
crown of lower Egypt with plumes and sundisk, see Ions (1968:87).

# Cats

Domestic cats and wild felines, notably lions, were a popular theme in Egyptian art; they were frequently depicted on wall murals and occasionally represented in tomb sculpture. Cats were associated with both the fierce lion-headed goddess Sekhmet and the benign cat-headed goddess Bastet; Egyptians made clear attributive and morphological distinctions between the two. Each deity was associated with opposing qualities of the sun: Sekhmet with its harsh, searing properties, and Bastet with its mild and useful heat. The bronze cat figures pictured here were undoubtedly made as votive images or accessories for the worship of Bastet, a primary center for which was located at Bubastis (modern Tell Basta).

The figure of the seated cat (cat. 58) is rendered in classic form with long front legs, a narrow body, a small head, and carefully delineated features. The figure is positioned on a thin base with a tang at the bottom that would have been used to secure it to a wooden base. Around its neck, the figure wears an incised and beaded choker from which an aegis of Bastet is suspended in the front; a counterpoise is positioned in the back. Jewelry depicted on cat bronzes was purely for the adornment of these cult statues; pet cats did not normally wear such jewelry. For similar bronze figures of seated cats, see Roeder (1956: abb. 50, 51) and Langton (1940: pl. II, III).

The posture of the crouching cat (cat. 57) was relatively rare among ancient Egyptian cat images, the upright seated position was much more common. Although overall details on this example are somewhat indistinct, it is possible to discern a small collar around the cat's neck. Tangs on the bottom indicate that it was secured to a larger base. For bronze figures of crouching cats, see Roeder (1956: abb. 480) and Langton (1940: pl. VI).

**57**
**Cat**
Third Intermediate Period (1085–715 BC)
Bronze
H: 1.5 in. (3.8 cm), L: 1.375 in. (3.5 cm)
Smith collection: *Bot of Dr. Banks, no. 219, Mar. 22, 1940 (15.–) Collection of 10 175.–*

**58** *(facing page)*
**Cat**
Third Intermediate Period (1085–715 BC)
Bronze
L: 3.3125 in. (8.4 cm)
Smith collection: *May 9, 1942 Bodley 67.50*

**59**
**Miniature sarcophagus for a snake**
Late Period (760–330 BC)
Bronze
H: 1.25 in. (3.2 cm), L: 2 in. (5.1 cm), W: 1 in. (2.5 cm)
Smith collection: *From private collection of the Duchess of Marlborough (Consuelo Vanderbilt) Bodley letter Aug. 11 '38 Bot of Bodley Book Shop, N.Y. cat. 243 Aug. 8 '39*
Consuelo Vanderbilt, the Duchess of Marlborough, traveled several times to Egypt, first in 1885, where she was "impressed by the magnificent proportions of the temples," though "the tombs... gave [her] the worst kind of claustrophobia and [she] was terrified by the hundreds of bats that clung to the low ceilings" (Balsan 1952:16).

Snakes were animals sacred to the god Atum, god of creation, and were depicted in votive images to the god. The animals were ritually sacrificed, mummified, and interred in special necropoli in Atum's city Heliopolis. Bronze snake sarcophagi ornamented with sculpted snake images such as the present example were more costly and thus would have conferred more prestige on the donor than would a mere mummified animal. For similar bronze snake sarcophagi, see Roeder (1956:386–7, pl. 55f).

**60**
**Uræus**
Late Period (760–330 BC)
Bronze
H: 3 in. (7.6 cm)
Ex collection F. G. Hilton Price
Paper labels: *URÆUS emblem of goddess- Tel. Basta.* and *232*; inscribed on bottom of marble base: *Tel Basta H. Price F. G. 1887*

This votive figure represents the rearing cobra with the crown of cow's horns and sun disk, worn by the goddesses Hathor and Isis. The six sections on the belly of the snake would have been inlaid with precious stones such as turquoise. See Roeder (1956:tafel 55) for similar crowned uræi with inlay. See also cat. 37 for a faience uræus amulet and further description of the figure, and see page 28 for a description of the Hilton Price collection.

# POTTERY FROM THE LEVANT

The first systematic excavations of pottery in the land of ancient Israel were conducted by W.M. Flinders Petrie in 1890, ten years after his first excavations in Egypt (Amiran 1969:13). Subsequent travelers to this region were interested in collecting and studying pottery from both Egypt and the Levant because of its connection to periods of biblical history.

Roman and pre-Roman pottery vessels, especially from Israel, are a rich source of information about the region's ancient cultures, especially concerning daily life. Pottery is also evidence of the inter-relation of ancient civilizations because it was traded and shipped over a wide area, as both end-product and as containers for goods of all types. The pottery vessels included here represent a sampling of some of the types of wares used in ancient Israel from early in the second millennium BC through Hellenistic and Roman times.

In addition to their utility in dating sites and cultures, many of the pottery pieces, especially the oil lamps, have an aesthetic component; some have decorative embellishments. The sequence of lamps, some of which have religious or cultural iconography, extends from the Hellenistic through the early Islamic period.

**61**
**Jug**
Iron IIA–B period (1000–700 BC)
Terra cotta
H: 4.25 in. (10.8 cm), D: 3.25 in. (8.3 cm)
Smith collection
Paper tag: *Iron II  Q 17 B 23/1/50 below foundation*

See Amiran (1969: pl. 86, no. 10–11) for classification of this type of jug with a rounded base, wide, slightly concave neck, and single handle. This example has five slightly raised parallel horizontal lines around the neck.

**62**
**Bowl**
Iron IIA–B period (1000–700 BC)
Terra cotta
H: 3.25 in. (8.3 cm), D: 7.5 in. (19.1 cm)
Smith collection

See Amiran (1969: pl. 62, no. 3–6) and Ackerman (1982: cat. 10) for examples of bowls with similar sharp carinated profiles and disk feet.

**63**
**Spouted vessel**
Iron IIA–B period (1000–700 BC)
Terra cotta
H: 5.75 in. (14.6 cm), W: 4.875 in. (12.4 cm)
Smith collection

**64**
**Jug**
Iron IIA–B period (1000–700 BC)
Terra cotta
H: 3.75 in. (9.5 cm), D: 2.375 in. (6 cm)
Smith collection
Paper tag: *Iron II  Nitla Trench 1 West 22.2.50*

See Amiran (1969: pl. 86, no. 10–11) for classification of this type of jug with a rounded base, wide, slightly concave neck, and single handle.

**65**

**Plate**

Iron IIC period (700–586 BC)

Terra cotta

D: 8 in. (20.3 cm)

Smith collection

See Ackerman (1982: cat. 24) for an example of a similar plate with a low disc base from a tomb in Lachish.

**66**

**Miniature beaker**

Persian period (586–332 BC)

Terra cotta

H: 4.75 in. (12.1 cm)

Smith collection

See Stern (1982: 126, fig. 201) and Curtis (1995: 155, no. 135) for similar examples of fine, small, pear-shaped beakers with bodies ending in a point.

**67**

**Juglet**

Iron IIC period (700–586 BC)

Terra cotta

H: 6 in. (15.2 cm)

Smith collection

This single-handled vessel is an example of a cylindrical dipper juglet. See Amiran (1969: 259, pl. 88, fig. 17) for classification of the type.

**68**

**Juglet**

Iron IIC period (700–586 BC)

Terra cotta

H: 3.75 in. (9.5 cm)

Smith collection

See Amiran for a similar example of a small black jug with a globular body (1969: 263, photo. 264) and for the classification of the type (Ibid.: pl. 89, no. 22).

**69**

**Beaker**

Iron IIC period (700–586 BC)

Terra cotta

H: 4.25 in. (10.8 cm), W: 4 in. (10.2 cm)

Smith collection

See Amiran (1969: pl. 99, no. 5) and Curtis (1995: 154, no. 129) for examples of this type of wide-rimmed beakers with bulbous bodies that taper to a point.

**70**
**Two-handled flagon**
Early Roman period (circa 37 BC–132 AD)
Terra cotta
H: 9 in. (22.9 cm), W: 3 in. (7.6 cm)
Smith collection

This flagon has two strap-like handles, a rim with a molding
pattern, and a slightly turned in mouth. The low foot has a slightly
recessed underside.

**71**
**Piriform bottle**
Early Roman period (circa 37 BC–132 AD)
Terra cotta
H: 7.75 in. (19.7 cm)
Smith collection

**72**
**Piriform bottle**
Early Roman period (circa 37 BC–132 AD)
Terra cotta
H: 4.5 in. (11.4 cm)
Smith collection

These two pear-shaped vessels were probably used for oils or scents.
Cat. 72 has a particularly nice rounded body and a gently flaring
rim. See Ackerman (1982: 114, cat. 111, 112) for similar examples.

**73**
**Oil lamp**
Early Roman period (circa 50 BC–140 AD)
Terra cotta
L: 3.5 in. (8.9 cm)
Smith collection

This small Herodian lamp has an unusual shape with a flat rim surrounded by an outside ridge, and a pattern of two circles above the nozzle. See Rosenthal (1978:80–1, fig. 333) for a similar lamp.

**74**
**Oil lamp**
Late Hellenistic period (167–37 BC)
Terra cotta
L: 3.5 in. (8.9 cm)
Smith collection

This is a provincial version of late Hellenistic ceramic lamps, with radiating lines as raised ridges on the rim.

**75**
**Oil lamp**
Early Islamic period (circa 7th century AD)
Terra cotta
L: 4 in. (10.2 cm)
Smith collection
Paper label: *Arabic ~~Roman~~ lamp pool of Bethesda 1938*

**76**
**Oil lamp**
Byzantine period (6th century AD)
Terra cotta
L: 4 in. (10.2 cm)
Smith collection

A Greek inscription surrounds the reservoir of this slipper-shaped lamp. See Kennedy (1963:pl. 26) for different varieties of this type.

**77**
**Oil lamp**
Byzantine period (3rd–6th century AD)
Terra cotta
L: 3.75 in. (9.5 cm)
Smith collection

This slipper-shaped lamp has a cross on the neck and a design of radial strokes in relief on the resevoir. See Kennedy (1963:cat. 640, pl. 25) for comparable examples.

**78**
**Oil lamp**
Roman period (1st–3rd century AD)
Terra cotta
L: 3.5 in. (8.9 cm)
Smith collection

A head of Medusa and other designs decorate this round lamp with a flat reservoir and small round nozzle.

# Mesopotamian Artifacts

One of the first writing systems, cuneiform, was developed by the cultures of ancient Mesopotamia in the 4th millenium BC. Papyrus was not available in ancient Mesopotamia as it was in Egypt, so clay was used as a medium for writing; cuneiform was developed to be imprinted on clay tablets or cones, and later adapted for inscription on stone or metal. By the late 3rd century BC, Akkadian, the predominant language of the region, had become the international language of the ancient world; cuneiform-inscribed clay tablets have been found in Egypt, the Levant, Anatolia, Syria, Armenia, Mesopotamia, and Iran (André-Leichnam in Boulanger 1982: 115).

The most ancient Mesopotamian objects presented here are mosaic cones dating to the Proto-Literate Period, circa 3200–2900 BC; they do not have inscriptions and were used purely for building decoration. The larger clay cones with inscriptions were made for Neo-Sumerian city-state kings from 2150 to 1870 BC. They belong to a corpus of cuneiform clay documents through which the history of these ancient civilizations has been preserved. They are identified with the reigns of Lipit-Eštar, King of Isin; Sin-kašid, King of Uruk; Gudea, King of Lagaš; and Nammahni, also King of Lagaš. Multiple cones, inscribed by hand, were ceremonially inserted into the walls of public buildings with the inscriptions visible only to the all-seeing divinity they addressed. In later periods, the circular ends were ornamented with inscriptions to be viewed by the public.

By the time of King Ashurbanipal in the Neo-Assyrian period (circa 7th century BC), when the molded plaque figures (cats. 91–2) were made, cuneiform was in the process of being superseded by the phonetic alphabet in many of these areas (Roaf 1990: 151). The plaque figures, from the Neo-Assyrian period (9th–7th century BC), were placed within the foundations of private buildings or residences, and had a protective function.

**79–85**
**Mosaic cones**
Proto-Literate Period (circa 3200–2900 BC)
Clay, some with pigment
L: 3.25–4.5 in. (8.3–11.4 cm)
Smith collection: *Tessallae, 8. Also 4 from E.S.S.* [E. S. Smith, A. Margurite Smith's sister] *Dug up by guard at base of Ziggurat at Ur in 1938*

These cones were used in architectural decoration; they were inserted into walls, with the circular painted ends visible, and arranged to create mosaics.

**86**
**Inscribed cone**
1934–1924 BC
Clay
L: 4.25 in. (10.8 cm)
Smith collection: *Bot of Dr. Banks, Oct. '35   15.-*

This cone has a thirty-six-line inscription of King Lipit-Eštar, the King of Isin (1934–1924 BC), which is translated:

> *I, Lipit-Eštar, humble shepherd of Nippur, true farmer of Ur, unceasing (provider) for Eridu,* en *priest suitable for Uruk, king of Isin, king of the land of Sumer and Akkad, favourite of the goddess Eštar, fashioned a pair of pot stands, a gift (for) the hands of the gods Enlil and Ninlil, in Isin, the city of my kingship at the palace gate. I, Lipit-Eštar, son of the god Enlil, (did this) when I established justice in the land of Sumer and Akkad* (Frayne 1990:51 Lipit-Eštar E4.1.5.3).

**87**
**Inscribed cone**
1934–1924 BC
Clay
L: 4.5 in. (11.4 cm)
Smith collection: *Bot of Dr. Banks, no. 2, Aug. 27, 1937, 26.-*

This cone contains a twenty-one-line inscription of King Lipit-Eštar, which is translated:

> *I, Lipit-Eštar, humble shepherd of Nippur, true farmer of Ur, unceasing (provider) for Eridu, en priest fit for Uruk, king of Isin, king of the land of Sumer and Akkad, favourite of the goddess Inanna, when I established justice in the land of Sumer and Akkad, I built the 'House of Justice' by the irrigation canal, the pre-eminent place of the gods* (Frayne 1990:54 Lipit-Eštar E4.1.5.3).

The references to Lipit-Eštar's having "established justice" and "built the 'House of Justice'" is consistent with his best known achievement, an extensive codex, substantial fragments of which have survived. The epithets and hymnal titles given in the inscriptions are also found in the Prologue to his *Lawcode* (Kramer in Pritchard 1950:159–61). The code deals with financial transactions, including land use, boat leases, taxes, and marriage and inheritance laws. Lipit-Eštar's *Lawcode* preceded and was undoubtedly an important source for portions of the better known and more extensive codex by the Babylonian king Hammurabi (1792–1750 BC).

**88**
**Inscribed cone**
circa 1870 BC
Clay
L: 2.4 in. (6.1 cm)
Smith collection: *Bot of Dr. Banks, Mar. 16, 1937 $8.-*

This cone contains an eight-line inscription of King Sin-kašid, which is translated: *Sin-kašid, mighty man, King of Uruk, king of Amnanum, provider of Eanna, built his royal palace* (Frayne 1990: 447).

King Sin-kašid was the first ruler recorded during the 19th century BC in the city-state of Uruk. It is known that he was allied by marriage to Sumu-la-El, King of Babylon, and that he was involved in a blockade of the Euphrates River, baring commerce between the rival city-states of Larsa to the south and Nippur to the north. His reign probably dates to 1870 BC (Roaf 1990: 112).

**89**
**Inscribed cone**
circa 2150 BC
Clay
L: 3 in. (7.6 cm)
Smith collection: *David, Feb. '48  15.-*

This cone contains a three-line inscription of King Nammahni, which is translated: *Nammahni, King of Lagaš* [author's translation after Steible (1991: 384)].

Very little is known concerning the reign of Nammahni of Lagaš. His dates are uncertain, but as he preceded the famed Gudea with one intervening ruler, he was probably in power around 2150 BC. It is known that Nammahni married the daughter of his predecessor Ur Bau and that he and Ur Bau's son, En-an-ni-pa (d)-da, may both have had status and influence in neighboring Ur (Pallis 1941: 209, 371, 381).

**90**
**Inscribed cone**
2144–2124 BC
Clay
L: 4.5 in. (11.4 cm)
Smith collection

This cone contains a ten-line inscription of King Gudea, which is translated:

> For Ningirsu, the powerful hero of Enlil, Gudea, king of Lagaš, made the necessary manifest, [he] has for him [i.e. Ningirsu] his Eninnu white Anzu [temple] built (and has [it]) for him restored [author's translation after Steible (1991:310)].

King Gudea (2144–2124 BC), one of the most famous of the Neo-Babylonian kings, ruled the city state of Lagaš during the period of the collapse of the Akkad empire. Although he is known to have conquered the Anshan and Elam peoples and possibly Ur as well, his reign is best known for stimulating a florescence of trade, culture, and architecture; he built and rebuilt at least thirteen temples.

This inscription records his restoration and further reconstruction of the Eninnu "white" temple of Ningirsu, the patron god of Lagaš. White Temples of this period owed their luster to gypsum plaster, which was used to coat the exterior walls (Roaf 1990: 62). King Gudea's gypsum-plastered temple is well documented. It was built with a dazzling array of materials, including cedar, gold, ivory and semi-precious stones, imported from distant lands (Barton in Prichard 1950: 268–9). For a stone portrait of Gudea with a drafting board on his knees showing the temple plan, see Du Ry (1969: 75).

**91**
**Plaque figure**
Neo-Assyrian period (9th–7th century BC)
Clay
L: 4.875 in. (12.4 cm), W: 2.125 in. (5.4 cm)
Smith collection

**92**
**Plaque figure**
Neo-Assyrian period (9th–7th century BC)
Clay
L: 4.375 in. (11.1 cm), W: 2.25 in. (5.7 cm)
Smith collection: *Bot of Dr. Banks, no. 10, Nov. 8, 1937 25.-*

The placement of plaque images in foundation deposits was
believed to protect the residents from evil demons and illness during the Neo-Assyrian period (Black and Green 1992:115). Cat.91
has been molded with the image of the protective deity Lahmu,
the male counterpart of the female primordial deity Lahamu.
Both Lahmu and Lahamu figured in the Babylonian story of creation. The name Lahmu means "hairy," referring to his long hair
and beard. For a similar inscribed plaque image that was found in
a vault within the foundations of a building at Aššur, see Black
and Green (1992:17, pl.9).

Cat.92 has the image of a sage or *apkallu*. Dressed in a fish costume
and carrying a bucket, he was believed to represent a supernatural
being (Black and Green 1992:83). Images of this sage, also with fish
costume and bucket, were recorded by Layard at Nimrud, "placed
at right angles to the entrance"(1853:289–90). The placement of
these specific figures flanking entrances and the discovery of slab
sculptures, like the present example, beneath building floors,
suggests the protective or auspicious function of the plaque images
of the fish-costumed sage (Black and Green 1992:83).

# Chronology of Egyptian History

**Paleolithic period** (700,000–5500 BC)

**Neolithic period** (5500–3000 BC)
Naqada I, Amratian Period (4000–3500 BC)
Naqada II, Early Gerzean Period (3500–3300 BC)
Naqada III, Late Gerzean Period (3300–3100 BC)

**Early Dynastic Period**
Dynasty 1 (3100–2890 BC)
Dynasty 2 (2890–2686 BC)

**Old Kingdom**
Dynasty 3 (2686–2613 BC)
Dynasty 4 (2613–2494 BC)
Dynasty 5 (2494–2345 BC)
Dynasty 6 (2345–2181 BC)
Dynasty 7 (2181–2173 BC)
Dynasty 8 (2173–2160 BC)

**First Intermediate Period**
Dynasties 9–10 (2160–2040 BC)
Pre-Unification Dynasty 11 (2133–2040 BC)

**Middle Kingdom**
Post–Unification Dynasty 11 (2040–1991 BC)
Dynasty 12 (1991–1786 BC)
Dynasty 13 (1786–1633 BC)

**Second Intermediate Period**
Dynasty 14 (1786–1603 BC)
Dynasties 15–16, Hyksos (1674–1558 BC)
Dynasty 17, Theban (1650–1558 BC)

**New Kingdom**
Dynasty 18, Thutmosid (1558–1303 BC)
Dynasty 19, First Ramesside Dynasty (1303–1200 BC)
Dynasty 20, Second Ramesside Dynasty (1200–1085 BC)

**Third Intermediate Period**
Dynasty 21, Tanite (1085–945 BC)
Dynasties 22–23, Bubastite (945–730 BC)
Dynasty 24, Pre-Saite (730–715 BC)

**Late Period**
Dynasty 25, Kushite (760–656 BC)
Dynasty 26, Saite (664–525 BC)
Dynasty 27, First Persian Domination (525–404 BC)
Dynasty 28 (404–398 BC)
Dynasty 29 (398–378 BC)
Dynasty 30 (378–341 BC)
Dynasty 31, Second Persian Domination  (341–330 BC)

**Conquest of Alexander the Great** (332 BC)

**Macedonian Domination** (332–304 BC)

**Ptolemaic Period** (304–30 BC)

**Roman Conquest** (30 BC)

**Roman Period** (30 BC–450 AD)

*All dates are approximate. Source: Scott 1986*

# BIBLIOGRAPHY

**Ackerman, Andrew and Susan L. Braunstein**
1982    *Israel in Antiquity*. New York: The Jewish Museum.

**Aldred, C.**
1971    *Jewels of the Pharoahs*. New York: Praeger Publishers.

**Alexander, Karen**
1994    "A History of the Ancient Art Collection at The Art Institute of Chicago" in *Ancient Art at The Art Institute of Chicago Museum Studies* 20, no. 1:7–13

**Allen, Thomas George**
1960    *The Egyptian Book of the Dead Documents in the Oriental Institute Museum at the University of Chicago*. Chicago: The University of Chicago Press.
1974    *The Book of the Dead or Going forth by Day*. Chicago: The University of Chicago Press.

**Amiran, Ruth**
1969    *Ancient Pottery of the Holy Land*. New Brunswick, NJ: Rutgers University Press.

**Andrews, Carol**
1994    *Amulets of Ancient Egypt*. London: British Museum Press.

**Arslan, Ermanno A., ed.**
1997    *Iside: Il Mito Il Mistero La Magia*. Milan: Electa.

**Aubert, J.-F. and L.**
1974    *Statuettes Égyptiennes, Chaouabtis, Ouchebities*. Paris: Librairie d'Amerique et d'Orient Adrien Maisonneure.

**Balsan, Consuleo Vanderbilt**
1952    *The Glitter and the Gold*. New York: Harper & Brothers Publishers.

**Ben Tor, D**.
1989    *The Scarab*. Tel Aviv: Sabinsky Press, Ltd.

**Black, Jeremy and Anthony Green**
1992    *Gods, Demons and Symbols of Ancient Mesopotamia An Illustrated Dictionary*. London: British Museum Press.

**Boulanger, Jean Paul**
1982    *Naissance de L'Écriture: Cunéiformes et Hiéroglpyhes*. Paris: Ministère de la Culture.

**Bourriau, Janine**
1988    *Pharaohs and Mortals: Egyptian Art in the Middle Kingdom*. Cambridge: Fitzwilliam Museum.

**British Museum**
1975    *Introductory Guide to the Egyptian Collections*. Cambridge: British Museum Publications, Ltd.

**Breasted, J.H., Jr.**
1948    *Egyptian Servant Statues*, The Bollingen Series XIII. Washington DC: Pantheon Books.

**Brovarski, Edward, Susan K. Doll, and Rita E. Freed, eds.**
1982    *Egypt's Golden Age: The Art of Living in the New Kingdom 1558–1085 B.C.* Boston: Museum of Fine Arts.

**Capel, Anne K. and Glenn E. Markoe, eds.**
1996    *Mistress of the House, Mistress of Heaven: Women in Ancient Egypt*. New York: Hudson Hills Press.

**Celenko, Theodore, ed.**
1996    *Egypt in Africa*. Indianapolis: Indianapolis Museum of Art

**Chappaz, J.-L.**
1984    *Les Figurines Funéraires Égyptiennes du Musée D'Art et D'Histoire et de Quelques Collections Privées*. Genéve: Musee d'art et d'historie de Genéve.

**Curtis, J.E. and J.E. Reade, eds.**
1995    *Art and Empire: Treasures from Assyria in the British Museum*. New York: Metropolitan Museum of Art.

**D'Auria, Sue, Peter Lacovara, and Catharine H. Roehrig, eds.**
1988    *Mummies and Magic: The Funerary Arts of Ancient Egypt*. Boston: Museum of Fine Arts.

**de Bernardy, Françoise**
1957    *Alexandre Walewski (1810–1868) Le fils Pononais de Napoléon*. Conde-sur-Escaut: Librarie Académique Perrin.

**Dunham, D.**
1937    "Introduction to Bronze Statuettes of Egypt" in *Buffalo Fine Arts Academy Master Bronzes*. Buffalo: Burrow and Company, Inc.

**Du Ry, Carel J.**
1969    *Art of the Ancient Near and Middle East*. New York: Harry N. Abrams, Inc.

**Frayne, Douglas**
1990    *Old Babylonian Period (2003–1595 BC)* in *The Royal Inscriptions of Mesopotamia, Early Periods* (vol. 4). Toronto: University of Toronto Press

**Garstant, John A.**
1907    *The Burial Customs of Ancient Egypt as Illustrated by Tombs of the Middle Kingdom*. London: A. Constable and Co., Ltd.

**Green, B.A.**
1989    *Ancient Egyptian Stone Vessels: Materials and Forms*. UMI Dissertation Services.

**Hayes, W.C.**
1978    *Scepter of Egypt*. (vols. I, II) New York: Mariden Grauvrelo.

**Haynes, Joyce**
1996    Unpublished manuscript.

**Hilton Price, F. G.**
1897    *A Catalogue of the Antiquities in the Possession of F. G. Hilton Price, Dir. S A.* (vol.1). London: Bernard Quaritch.

**Ions, Veronica**
1968 [1965]    *Egyptian Mythology*. Feltham: The Hamlyn Publishing Group Ltd.

**Kennedy, Charles A.**
1963    "The Development of the Lamp in Palestine." *Berytins* 14:67–115.

**Langton, N. & B.**
1940    *The Cat in Ancient Egypt*. Cambridge: Cambridge University Press.

**Layard, Austin H.**
1853    *Discoveries Among the Ruins of Nineveh and Babylon; with Travels in Armenia, Kurdistan, and the Desert: Being the Result of a Second Expedition Undertaken for the Trustees of the British Museum*. New York: G.P. Putnam & Co.

**Lucas, Alfred**
1962    *Ancient Egyptian Materials and Industries*, 4th ed. (rev. and enlarged by J.R. Harris) London: E. Arnold.

**Lurker, Manfred**
1986 [1980]    *The Gods and Symbols of Ancient Egypt*. Trans. Barbara Cummings. London: Thames & Hudson, Ltd.

**Malek, Jaromir**
1993    *The Cat in Ancient Egypt.*
Philadelphia: University of
Pennsylvania Press.

**Moscati, Sabatino, ed.**
1988    *The Phoenicians.* Milan:
Bompiani.

**National Geographic**
1978    *Ancient Egypt: Discovering
its Splendors.* Washington DC:
National Geographic Society.

**Newberry, P.**
1957    "Funerary Statuettes"
in *Cairo Catalogue General.* Cairo:
L'Institute Francais d'Archéologie
Orientale.

**Pallis, Svend Aagge**
1941    *Chronology of the Shub-Ad
Culture.* Copenhagen: Povl
Branner.

**Petrie, W. M. Flinders**
1890    *Kahun, Gurob, and Hawara.*
London: Kegan Paul, Trench,
Trübner, and Co.
1896    *Naquada.* London: B.
Quaritch.
1914a    *Amulets: Illustrated by the
Egyptian Collection in University
College, London.* London:
Constable & Company, Ltd.
1914b    *Shabtis: Illustrated by the
Egyptian Collection in the University
College, London.* London: British
School of Egyptian Archaeology.

**Pritchard, James B. ed.**
1950    *Ancient Near Eastern
Texts Relating to the Old Testament.*
Princeton: Princeton University
Press.

**Ranke, Hermann**
1935    *Die Ägyptischen
Personannamen* I. Glückstadt:
J.-J. Augustin.

**Reeves, N.**
1984    "Excavations in the Valley
of the Kings" in *Mitteilungen des
Deutschen Archaologischen Institut
Abteilung Kairo* 40: 227–235.

**Reisner, G.A.**
1907    *Amulets.* CCG I, II. Cairo:
L'Institut Francais d'Archéologie
Orientale.

**Roaf, Michael**
1990    *Mesopotamia and the Ancient
Near East.* Oxford: Equinox, Ltd.

**Roeder, G.**
1956    *Ägyptische Bronzefiguren.*
Berlin: Staatliche Museen zu
Berlin.

**Romano, James F.**
1982    "Kohl and Kohl
Containers" in *Egypt's Golden
Age: The Art of Living in the New
Kingdom 1158–1085 BC.* Edward
Brovarski, Susan K. Doll, and
Rita E. Freed, eds. Boston:
Museum of Fine Arts.

**Rosenthal, Renate and Renee
Sivan**
1978    "Ancient Lamps in the
Schloessinger Collection."
*Qedem* 8.

**Roth, A.M. and C.H. Roehrig**
1989    "The Bersheh Procession:
A New Reconstruction." *Journal of
the Museum of Fine Arts, Boston*
1: 31–40.

**Schneider, H.D.**
1977    *Shabtis: An Introduction to
the History of Ancient Egyptian
Funerary Statuettes with a Catalogue
of the Collection of Shabtis in the
National Museum of Antiquities at
Leiden* (3 volumes). Leiden:
Rijksmuseum van Oudheden.

**Scott, Gerry D.**
1986    *Ancient Egyptian Art at
Yale.* New Haven: Yale University
Art Gallery.

**Sotheby, Wilkinson & Hodge**
1911    *Catalogue of the Important
and Extensive Collection of Egyptian
Antiquities, The Property of the Late
F.G. Hilton-Price, Esq.* London:
Sotheby, Wilkinson & Hodge

**Spencer, A. J.**
1993    *Early Egypt: The Rise of
Civilization in the Nile Valley.*
Norman: University of
Oklahoma Press.

**Steible, Horst**
1991    *Die Neusumerischen Bau-
und Weihinschriften* in *Freiburger
Altorientalische Studien* (Band 9,1).
Stuttgart: Franz Steiner Verlag.

**Stern, Ephraim**
1982    *Material Culture of the Land
of the Bible in the Persian Period,
538–332 B.C.* Warmenster,
England: Aris & Phillips.

**Tomkins, Calvin**
1970    *Merchants and Masterpieces:
The Story of the Metropolitan Museum
of Art.* New York: E.P. Dutton &
Co., Inc.

**Tying, Rev. Stephen H.**
1875    *In Memoriam, William
Tilden Blodgett: Address of Rev.
Stephen H. Tying, D.D., on the
Occasion of the Funeral of William T.
Blodgett,* including the minutes of
the quarterly meeting of the
Trustees of the Metropolitan
Museum of Art, 15 November
1875. New York.

**Vercoutter, Jean, Jean Leclant,
Frank M. Snowden, Jr., and
Jehan Desanges**
1991[1976]    *The Image of the Black
in Western Art.* Vol. 1, *From the
Pharoahs to the Fall of the Roman
Empire.* Cambridge: Harvard
University Press.

**Wilkinson, A.**
1975    *Ancient Egyptian Jewelry.*
London: Methuen and Co., Ltd.

**Wilson, John A.**
1956[1951]    *The Culture of Ancient
Egypt.* Chicago: University of
Chicago Press.

**Winlock, Hebert Eustis**
1955    *Models of Daily Life in
Ancient Egypt from the Tomb of
Meket-Re at Thebes.* Cambridge:
Harvard University Press.

HURST GALLERY has been dealing art and artifacts of the Pacific, Africa, and the Americas, and Antiquities and Asian art, for twenty years. We are actively involved in appraising collections for both institutions and private clients. Our exhibitions are well attended and our catalogs are circulated worldwide. The gallery seeks significant collections or individual objects in any of the above-mentioned categories. Hurst Gallery offers experienced and specialized attention that is not available elsewhere.

## PUBLICATIONS FROM PAST EXHIBITIONS

**Ngola: The Weapon as Authority, Identity, and Ritual Object in Sub-Saharan Africa**
(1997) ISBN 0-9628074-6-X, text by Norman Hurst, 48 pages, fully illustrated with 12 color, 21 b/w photographs of 62 objects, map, bibliography, $20 domestic, $30 foreign

**Power and Prestige: The Arts of Island Melanesia and the Polynesian Outliers**
(1996) ISBN 0-9628074-5-1, text by Norman Hurst, 88 pages, fully illustrated with 42 color, 26 b/w photographs of 127 objects, maps, illustrations, extensive bibliography, $20 domestic, $30 foreign

**Collecting African Art: 1890s–1950s**
(1996) ISBN 0-9628074-4-3, text by Christa Clarke, 48 pages, fully illustrated with 21 color, 23 b/w photographs of 50 objects, extensive bibliography, $20 domestic, $30 foreign

**Art and Artifacts of Melanesia**
(1992) ISBN 0-9628074-3-5, 80 pages, 71 b/w photographs of 90 objects, maps, extensive bibliography, $20 domestic, $30 foreign

**Native American Basketry**
(1992) ISBN 0-9628074-2-7, text by Sarah Peabody Turnbaugh, 56 pages, 37 b/w photographs of 98 baskets, maps, bibliography, $15 domestic, $20 foreign

**Visual Diplomacy: The Art of the Cameroon Grassfields**
(1991) ISBN 0-9628074-1-9, text by Marcilene Keeling Wittmer, 32 pages, 26 b/w photographs of 30 objects, map, illustrations, bibliography, $15 domestic, $20 foreign

**Art and Artifacts of Polynesia**
(1990) ISBN 0-9628074-0-0, text by Anne D'Alleva, 64 pages, 12 color and 32 b/w photographs of 78 objects, maps, bibliography, $20 domestic, $30 foreign

**The Ancient Southwest**
(1989) 48 pages, 1 color and 49 b/w photographs of 105 objects, maps, $15 domestic, $20 foreign

Out of print catalogues available as photocopied black & white facsimiles for $10 each:
**African Arts of War and Peace** (1988) 48 pages, 73 b/w photographs
**Art of New Guinea** (1988) 52 pages, 2 color and 101 b/w photographs, maps, bibliography
**Art of Polynesia** (1987) 50 pages, 2 color and 92 b/w photographs, bibliography
**Polynesia: Objects of Daily Life** (1985) 32 pages, 34 b/w photographs
**Art of the Negritos** (1987) 44 pages, 78 b/w photographs, map, bibliography
**Art of West Africa** (1987) 28 pages, 36 b/w photographs

(all prices include postage and handling)